Smart Grid Cybersecurity: Attacking and Defending Energy IoT Systems

Zephyrion Stravos

I have a confession. I get a strange thrill out of breaking things—digitally, of course. There's something exhilarating about poking at a system, peeling back its layers, and uncovering the cracks hidden beneath all that shiny, well-marketed security. If you're holding this book, I have a feeling you might be the same. Welcome, fellow troublemaker (the good kind, I hope), to **Smart Grid Cybersecurity: Attacking and Defending Energy IoT Systems**—where we dive into the fascinating, often terrifying, world of energy infrastructure hacking.

This book is part of my *IoT Red Teaming: Offensive and Defensive Strategies series*, which, if you haven't checked out already, is a glorious buffet of cyber mayhem. Whether you want to hack smart vehicles (The Car Hacker's Guide), play with medical devices (Hacking Medical IoT), or even mess with space (Satellite Hacking), we've got you covered. But today, we're not dealing with self-driving cars or pacemakers. No, today we set our sights on something bigger. Much bigger.

We're talking about the smart grid—the lifeblood of modern civilization. You like lights? Refrigerators? Charging your phone so you can endlessly scroll memes? All of that relies on one thing: electricity. And as much as we'd like to think our power grid is an impenetrable fortress, the reality is, it's more like a house of cards balanced on a wobbly table during an earthquake.

Wait, the Power Grid Can Be Hacked?

Oh, absolutely. And it has been. Ever heard of BlackEnergy? Industroyer? Stuxnet? If not, buckle up, because we're going to be talking about how real-world cyberattacks have already turned off the lights in entire countries. And before you ask—yes, the possibility of someone hacking the grid and sending us all back to the Stone Age is very real. In fact, it's not even that hard.

Why? Because the power grid is old. I mean, really old. Picture a geriatric IT guy still using a Windows XP machine to control nuclear reactors, and you're not far off. Many of the critical infrastructure systems we rely on were designed before the internet was a thing. So naturally, when we started connecting them to the internet (because of course we did), we created an attack surface the size of Texas.

But here's the kicker: we didn't stop at just making the grid digital—we made it smart. And by "smart," I mean "full of internet-connected devices that hackers love to play with."

The Smart Grid: A Hacker's Playground

The smart grid is like the internet of things (IoT) on steroids. It's packed with smart meters, SCADA systems, edge computing nodes, and wireless communication networks. If that all sounds like tech jargon, don't worry—we're going to break it down. But the important thing to know is that every smart component added to the grid is a new attack vector waiting to be exploited.

Imagine this: a cybercriminal (or a rogue nation-state, if we're feeling dramatic) gets access to a few thousand smart meters. They launch a coordinated attack that manipulates energy consumption data, causing mass billing fraud, or worse—an entire city suddenly loses power. Or maybe they find a vulnerability in EV charging infrastructure, leading to massive disruptions in transportation.

These aren't just hypotheticals. Attacks like this have already happened, and it's only going to get crazier as the grid becomes even smarter.

Who Is This Book For?

Maybe you're an ethical hacker, penetration tester, or cybersecurity researcher looking to understand how to break (and fix) critical infrastructure. Maybe you work in the energy sector and want to know how to keep the bad guys from flipping your off switch. Or maybe you're just a cyber-curious soul who likes the idea of learning how hackers think. Whatever your reason, you're in the right place.

This book isn't just about how to attack smart grid systems—it's about how to defend them too. Because, let's be honest, while hacking is fun, keeping the lights on is kind of important.

What's Inside?

We're starting off with the basics—what makes up a smart grid, how its communication networks work, and what protocols keep everything running. Then, we're going full red-team mode:

- **Reconnaissance and attack surface mapping** – Finding and identifying vulnerable devices (Shodan fans, you'll love this one).
- **Exploiting Advanced Metering Infrastructure (AMI)** – Because smart meters are way more fun when you can manipulate energy readings.
- **Attacking SCADA and Industrial Control Systems (ICS)** – Learn why outdated protocols and unsecured remote access make these systems hacker candy.

- **Wireless and RF hacking** – Because Zigbee, LoRa, and 5G are not as secure as vendors want you to believe.
- **Hacking EV charging infrastructure** – Because the future of transportation should not come with built-in security nightmares.
- **Cyber-physical attacks and blackout scenarios** – This is where things get real.

And finally, how to defend against all of this madness, because as much as we love a good exploit, keeping critical infrastructure secure is kinda important.

Why Should You Listen to Me?

Great question. I'm Zephyrion Stravos—cybersecurity researcher, hacker, and general breaker-of-things. If you've read any of the other books in the IoT Red Teaming series, you know that I like to dive deep into the mechanics of hacking while keeping things fun. Because let's be honest—cybersecurity books can be painfully dry, and I refuse to subject you to that.

This book is going to be informative, yes, but it's also going to be a ride. Expect war stories, ridiculous real-world failures, and plenty of moments where you'll be thinking, Wait… people actually deployed this in production?

Final Warning: Don't Be a Villain

I shouldn't have to say this, but I will—this book is for educational purposes only. If you're reading this because you want to go out and cause chaos, let me stop you right there. Real hackers, the good ones, understand that with great power comes great responsibility (yes, I just quoted Spider-Man).

Use this knowledge to protect, defend, and make the grid stronger—not to send us all back to the dark ages.

Alright, enough talk. Let's get to the fun stuff.

Chapter 1: Introduction to Smart Grid Security

Picture this: You're cozied up on your couch, lights on, fridge humming, phone charging—and boom! Darkness. Not because you forgot to pay your electric bill, but because some hacker halfway across the world decided to flip the switch on your entire city. Fun, right? The smart grid, for all its high-tech marvels, is riddled with vulnerabilities that make hackers salivate. And while most people think of cyberattacks as something that affects their email or bank accounts, the reality is far scarier—someone, somewhere, could be plotting a blackout just for kicks (or worse, for ransom). Welcome to the wild world of smart grid security, where the stakes aren't just data breaches but full-blown power grid meltdowns.

The smart grid is an interconnected network of power generation, distribution, and consumption technologies designed to improve efficiency, reliability, and sustainability. It integrates IoT devices, SCADA systems, AMI networks, and advanced communication protocols to modernize energy delivery. However, this increased connectivity also expands the attack surface, making the grid susceptible to cyber threats. This chapter provides an overview of the smart grid ecosystem, key vulnerabilities, major cyber threats, and regulatory frameworks such as NERC CIP, IEC 62443, and ISO 27019 that aim to safeguard critical infrastructure.

1.1 Understanding the Smart Grid Ecosystem and Components

Alright, let's start with a simple question: What's the worst thing that could happen if someone hacks the power grid? If your answer was "a few lights go out," oh buddy, you're in for a ride. Because the reality is far worse. Imagine hospitals shutting down, traffic lights going haywire, factories grinding to a halt, and people losing their minds because they can't charge their smartphones.

That's why the smart grid exists—to make our energy infrastructure more efficient, reliable, and "intelligent." But, as with all things IoT, the smarter it gets, the more hackable it becomes. Before we start breaking things (ethically, of course), we first need to understand what we're dealing with. Let's take a deep dive into what makes up the smart grid and why securing it is like trying to guard an open vault with a sign that says "Please don't steal."

What Exactly is a Smart Grid?

Imagine the traditional power grid as a one-way street—electricity flows from power plants to consumers, and that's about it. Now, enter the smart grid, which turns that one-way street into a chaotic, two-way highway with real-time data, automation, and IoT devices running the show.

In simple terms, a smart grid is just a digitally enhanced version of our old-school power grid. It uses IoT sensors, automation, and AI-driven analytics to monitor, control, and optimize energy distribution. The goal? Better efficiency, fewer blackouts, and lower energy costs. Sounds great, right? Well, it is—until someone hacks it.

To really understand why the smart grid is both amazing and terrifying, we need to break it down into its key components.

Key Components of the Smart Grid

The smart grid is like a giant, complex puzzle made up of various interconnected parts. Here's a rundown of the most important ones:

1. Power Generation (The Source of It All)

This is where electricity is produced—power plants, renewable energy sources (solar, wind, hydro), and even small-scale distributed energy resources (DERs) like rooftop solar panels. The modern grid allows energy to flow not just from big power plants, but also from consumers who generate their own electricity.

Security Risk: Many power generation systems still rely on outdated industrial control systems (ICS) and SCADA networks, making them vulnerable to cyberattacks. (Remember Stuxnet? Yeah, that wasn't just a movie plot.)

2. Transmission Networks (The Highways of Electricity)

Once power is generated, it needs to be transported over high-voltage transmission lines to substations. This is where SCADA (Supervisory Control and Data Acquisition) systems come in, allowing operators to monitor and control power flow.

Security Risk: SCADA systems were never designed with security in mind. Many still run on default passwords, and some are even connected to the internet (because why not make a hacker's job easier, right?).

3. Substations (The Traffic Controllers)

Think of substations as the middlemen in the energy world. They step down high-voltage electricity into lower voltages before sending it to homes and businesses. Modern substations are fully automated, using IoT sensors and communication networks to self-heal during faults.

Security Risk: Attackers can remotely manipulate circuit breakers to cause blackouts or fry transformers with well-crafted cyberattacks. Ever heard of Industroyer? It was designed to do just that.

4. Distribution Networks (Getting Power to Your Home)

From substations, power is distributed through lower-voltage lines to homes, businesses, and industries. Smart grids use Advanced Metering Infrastructure (AMI) to monitor real-time electricity usage and allow utilities to control power delivery remotely.

Security Risk: Smart meters can be hacked to manipulate billing data, cause power outages, or even create botnets for larger cyberattacks. Yes, your smart meter could be part of the next DDoS attack on a power grid.

5. Smart Meters (Big Brother in Your Home?)

Smart meters are the IoT devices of the energy world. They measure real-time electricity consumption, send data to utility companies, and even allow for remote power shut-off.

Security Risk: If compromised, smart meters can be used for billing fraud, power theft, or large-scale coordinated attacks. Oh, and in case you were wondering—yes, hackers have already found ways to manipulate them.

6. Grid Edge Computing (Where the Magic Happens)

The smart grid isn't just about sending electricity—it's also about processing insane amounts of data in real time. Grid edge computing allows data to be analyzed closer to the source, reducing latency and improving decision-making.

Security Risk: Anything connected to the internet is a target, and grid edge devices run software that can be exploited just like any other IoT system. Expect firmware attacks, malware, and ransomware threats.

The Smart Grid: A Cybersecurity Nightmare?

At this point, you're probably thinking, Wow, this is just a giant network of vulnerable IoT devices with a power supply attached! And you'd be absolutely right.

The smart grid's reliance on real-time data, remote access, and IoT connectivity makes it an ideal target for cybercriminals. From nation-state attackers to script kiddies messing around with open-source tools, everyone wants a piece of the action.

Some of the biggest cybersecurity risks include:

- Ransomware attacks on utilities (because nothing says "pay up" like shutting off the power to a major city)
- Supply chain vulnerabilities (hacking third-party vendors to get inside critical systems)
- Wireless protocol exploits (hijacking Zigbee, LoRa, and 5G communications)
- Man-in-the-middle (MITM) attacks (intercepting and manipulating grid data)

If the idea of power grid cyberattacks wasn't already keeping you up at night, well… sorry about that.

Final Thoughts: Welcome to the Jungle

The smart grid is an engineering marvel, but it's also a cybersecurity minefield. The more we automate, digitize, and connect, the more doors we open for attackers. Understanding its components is the first step in securing it—because trust me, the bad guys are already doing their homework.

So, what's next? In the coming chapters, we'll map out attack surfaces, break into SCADA systems, and hack (and secure) smart meters. Think of this as your crash course in defending modern civilization—because let's be real, without electricity, we're all just a bunch of people sitting in the dark, staring at useless Wi-Fi routers.

Let's make sure that doesn't happen. Onward to the next chapter!

1.2 Attack Surfaces in Smart Grid Infrastructure

Alright, let's play a quick game. Imagine you're a hacker (a legal, ethical one, of course) trying to mess with the power grid. Where would you start? Would you try hacking a smart meter to change your electricity bill to zero? Maybe spoof SCADA system data so operators think everything is fine—right before you plunge a city into darkness? Or perhaps you'd go after wireless communication channels and jam critical signals?

If you answered all of the above, congratulations! You have the right hacker mindset— because in the world of smart grids, there isn't just one attack surface. There are dozens, each one a potential entry point for cybercriminals. From hardware vulnerabilities to wireless exploits, smart grids are full of security holes just waiting to be discovered (and patched, hopefully).

So, let's dig into the attack surfaces of smart grid infrastructure—the digital doors hackers are constantly trying to break down.

What Is an Attack Surface?

Before we start hacking (theoretical hacking, of course), let's define what an attack surface actually is.

An attack surface refers to all the possible entry points that an attacker can exploit to compromise a system. In a traditional IT network, this could be open ports, unpatched software, weak credentials, or social engineering attacks. But in a smart grid, things get way more complicated because we're dealing with a mix of IT, OT (Operational Technology), IoT, and wireless systems.

A smart grid's attack surface is massive, spanning:

- **Physical components** (power plants, substations, smart meters)
- **Communication networks** (wired and wireless protocols)
- **Software and applications** (SCADA, EMS, and utility management systems)
- **Human factors** (yes, people are always the weakest link)

Each of these presents a unique set of risks, and if you're thinking, Wow, this is a security nightmare, then you're absolutely right. Let's break it down piece by piece.

1. Physical Attack Surfaces: The Hands-On Approach

Most cyberattacks don't require physical access, but in the smart grid, physical security is just as important as cybersecurity. After all, if an attacker can physically tamper with a device, it's game over.

Common Physical Threats:

- **Tampering with smart meters** (modifying firmware to manipulate electricity bills)
- **Gaining unauthorized access to substations** (disrupting power distribution)
- **Planting rogue devices** (installing malicious hardware to eavesdrop on networks)
- **Stealing grid-edge computing devices** (exploiting stolen credentials and sensitive data)

Real-World Example:

Did you know that smart meters have been hacked to reduce electricity bills? Criminal groups in Europe and South America have been caught modifying meter firmware to report lower energy consumption—costing utility companies millions in lost revenue.

Defensive Strategy:

- Use tamper-proof smart meters with cryptographic authentication
- Deploy CCTV and motion sensors at substations and critical infrastructure
- Implement strong physical access controls (badges, biometrics, and multi-layer authentication)

2. Communication Networks: The Hacker's Playground

Smart grids rely on a mix of wired and wireless networks to transmit data between devices, control systems, and utility operators. But here's the problem—many of these communication protocols were never designed with security in mind.

Common Network Threats:

- **Man-in-the-Middle (MITM) attacks** (intercepting and modifying grid data)
- **Protocol spoofing** (faking SCADA commands to cause disruptions)
- **Wireless jamming** (disrupting AMI and IoT networks)
- **Replay attacks** (resending old commands to manipulate grid operations)

Real-World Example:

Remember BlackEnergy? This was the malware used in the 2015 Ukrainian power grid attack, which left 230,000 people without electricity. Attackers gained access to SCADA systems, remotely shut down circuit breakers, and even disabled backup power systems—all thanks to weak network security.

Defensive Strategy:

- Encrypt all network traffic (DNP3, IEC 61850, and Modbus should never be unencrypted)
- Use AI-powered anomaly detection to identify unauthorized activity
- Implement intrusion detection systems (IDS) and intrusion prevention systems (IPS)

3. Software and Application Attack Surfaces: Hacking the Brains of the Grid

Smart grids depend on a ton of software applications—from SCADA systems to energy management platforms. Unfortunately, many of these applications are outdated, poorly patched, or just badly designed from a security standpoint.

Common Software Threats:

- Exploiting unpatched vulnerabilities in SCADA and EMS software
- Injecting malware or ransomware into control systems
- Exploiting insecure APIs to gain unauthorized access
- Default or weak passwords (yes, "admin/admin" is still a thing)

Real-World Example:

In 2021, a hacker remotely accessed a water treatment plant in Florida using a default password and attempted to poison the water supply. Now, imagine if the same happened in a smart grid control center. Scary, right?

Defensive Strategy:

- Regularly update and patch SCADA software
- Implement strong authentication mechanisms (multi-factor authentication is a must)
- Audit APIs for security vulnerabilities before deployment

4. Human Attack Surfaces: The Weakest Link

No matter how advanced cybersecurity gets, humans will always be the weakest link. Social engineering, phishing, and insider threats are just as dangerous as technical exploits.

Common Human-Based Threats:

- Phishing attacks (tricking employees into revealing login credentials)
- Insider threats (disgruntled employees sabotaging grid systems)
- Social engineering (pretending to be an IT technician to gain access)

Real-World Example:

In 2017, hackers used phishing emails to infiltrate U.S. energy companies, gaining access to critical infrastructure networks. Sometimes, all it takes is one careless click.

Defensive Strategy:

- Conduct regular security awareness training for employees
- Implement zero-trust architecture (assume no one can be trusted by default)
- Use behavioral analytics to detect insider threats

Final Thoughts: So Many Holes, So Little Time

If the smart grid were a fortress, it would be one with hundreds of open doors, weak locks, and a neon sign that says "Hack Me." From physical attacks to network exploits, software vulnerabilities, and social engineering, attackers have too many ways to break in.

Securing the smart grid isn't just about patching software—it's about locking down every possible attack surface. Because at the end of the day, one weak link is all it takes to cause a major blackout.

So, what's next? In the following chapters, we'll start getting our hands dirty with reconnaissance, exploitation techniques, and defense strategies. Because knowing the attack surfaces is just the first step—now it's time to start hacking (and securing) the grid!

1.3 Key Cyber Threats in Energy IoT Systems

Alright, let's start with a question: What's scarier than a hacker in your smart home? A hacker in your entire power grid. Imagine waking up one day, flipping the switch, and—nothing happens. No Wi-Fi, no coffee maker, no charging your phone. Worse? Hospitals, traffic lights, water treatment plants—all offline. Suddenly, we're back in the stone age, except with a whole lot more panicked tweets (until phone batteries die, of course).

That's the nightmare scenario. But guess what? It's not just theoretical. Energy IoT systems—smart meters, industrial control systems (ICS), SCADA networks, EV charging stations, distributed energy resources (DERs)—are all under attack. And the threats? They're not just coming from lone hackers in basements. We're talking about organized cybercriminal groups, nation-state actors, ransomware gangs, and, occasionally, some kid on the internet proving a point.

So, what are the biggest cyber threats keeping grid operators, utility companies, and security professionals up at night? Let's dive in.

1. Nation-State Attacks: When Cyberwar Targets the Grid

One of the biggest threats to energy IoT systems isn't just random hackers—it's nation-states with armies of cyber warriors. Governments have realized that power grids are prime targets in cyber warfare. Why? Because taking down an enemy's power grid can cripple an entire country without firing a single bullet.

🔐 How Nation-State Attacks Work:

Advanced Persistent Threats (APTs): Nation-state hackers infiltrate grid networks slowly and stealthily, planting malware that remains dormant until needed.

Grid Manipulation: Attackers alter grid settings, trip circuit breakers, or overload transformers, causing massive blackouts.

Supply Chain Attacks: Instead of hacking the grid directly, attackers compromise hardware and software suppliers, injecting backdoors before equipment is even installed.

💡 Real-World Example:

The 2015 Ukraine Power Grid Attack—a sophisticated cyberattack attributed to Russian APT groups BlackEnergy and Sandworm—left 230,000 people without power for hours. Attackers gained access to SCADA systems, remotely shut down power stations, and even disabled backup systems.

♀ Defensive Strategy:

Isolate critical systems (air-gapping where possible).

Deploy network segmentation to prevent malware from spreading.

Regularly audit and update firmware/software for vulnerabilities.

2. Ransomware: Holding the Grid Hostage

If there's one thing cybercriminals love, it's ransomware. Why? Because locking down critical infrastructure means big paydays. Ransomware attacks on energy IoT systems can cripple utility companies, causing blackouts and forcing desperate organizations to pay millions in ransom.

☠ How Ransomware Works in Smart Grids:

Hackers infect grid control systems, encrypting critical files and demanding payment.

IoT devices like smart meters and grid sensors become attack vectors.

Ransomware-as-a-Service (RaaS) lets even low-level hackers launch attacks.

♀ Real-World Example:

The Colonial Pipeline ransomware attack (2021) shut down fuel supplies across the U.S. East Coast. A single compromised VPN password led to a $4.4 million ransom payment and nationwide fuel shortages.

♀ Defensive Strategy:

Implement strict backup policies to restore systems quickly.

Use AI-based anomaly detection to spot ransomware early.

Train employees on phishing and social engineering tactics.

3. Smart Meter Hacking: Fraud, Tampering, and Billing Exploits

Smart meters are one of the most widespread IoT devices in the energy sector. They track electricity usage, help manage demand, and eliminate the need for manual readings. But they also introduce massive security risks.

📹 Common Smart Meter Attacks:

Tampering with firmware to report lower electricity usage.

Man-in-the-Middle (MITM) attacks to alter data in transit.

Jamming wireless signals to prevent accurate readings.

🔑 Real-World Example:

In Spain, energy thieves hacked smart meters to reduce their bills, costing utility companies millions. Some even sold hacked meters on the black market, creating a full-blown fraud economy.

💡 Defensive Strategy:

Use cryptographic authentication in smart meters.

Regularly update meter firmware to patch vulnerabilities.

Deploy intrusion detection systems to spot anomalies.

4. EV Charging Station Exploits: Powering Up Cybercrime

With the rise of electric vehicles (EVs), charging stations have become a new attack surface. Since these stations connect to both the power grid and the internet, they present a juicy target for cybercriminals.

📹 How Hackers Exploit EV Chargers:

Hacking charge stations to steal personal and payment data.

Launching DDoS attacks to overload the grid.

Using vehicle-to-grid (V2G) exploits to manipulate power demand.

📍 Real-World Example:

In 2022, hackers remotely shut down charging stations in Russia, displaying anti-war messages on their screens. Imagine if attackers shut down entire networks of EV chargers in a country—total transportation chaos.

💡 Defensive Strategy:

Implement strong encryption for V2G communications.

Use secure boot mechanisms to prevent firmware tampering.

Deploy firewalls and network monitoring for charging stations.

5. Wireless and RF Attacks: The Silent Threat
Wireless technologies like Zigbee, LoRa, Wi-SUN, and 5G play a crucial role in the smart grid. But they also introduce radio frequency (RF) vulnerabilities that hackers can exploit without even touching a single device.

📻 Common RF-Based Attacks:

Jamming attacks to disrupt smart grid communication.

Replay attacks to send malicious commands.

Side-channel attacks to extract encryption keys.

📍 Real-World Example:

Researchers have demonstrated how LoRa-based smart meters can be jammed from over 1 km away, rendering them useless.

💡 Defensive Strategy:

Use spread spectrum and frequency hopping to counter jamming.

Implement cryptographic countermeasures against replay attacks.

Monitor RF signals for anomalies.

Final Thoughts: The Cyber Battle for the Grid

If you weren't paranoid before, you should be now. Energy IoT systems are under constant attack, from nation-state cyberwarfare to ransomware gangs and street-level fraudsters. Whether it's hacking smart meters, exploiting SCADA systems, or jamming wireless signals, the risks are very, very real.

But don't worry—we're not doomed yet. As attackers evolve, so do defensive strategies. The key is constant vigilance, proactive security, and a hacker mindset—because you can't defend against what you don't understand.

And with that, we're just getting started. Next up, we'll dive into regulations and compliance—aka, the rules that hopefully keep the grid from becoming the Wild West of cybercrime. Stay tuned! ⚡🖥️🔒

1.4 Regulations and Compliance Standards (NERC CIP, IEC 62443, ISO 27019)

Alright, time to talk about rules. I know, I know—regulations and compliance standards might not sound as thrilling as hacking a smart meter or taking over a SCADA system, but trust me, they matter.

Think of cybersecurity regulations as the seatbelt laws of the smart grid world. Sure, you could drive without a seatbelt, but the first time you crash (or in this case, get hit by a cyberattack), you'll wish you followed the rules. And in the energy sector, a "crash" doesn't just mean a few lost emails—it means blackouts, financial losses, and possibly national security disasters.

So, if you work in smart grid security, you need to know the major compliance standards: NERC CIP (North America), IEC 62443 (global industrial cybersecurity), and ISO 27019 (information security for energy). These aren't just bureaucratic red tape—they set the minimum security requirements to protect power grids from hackers, cybercriminals, and even rogue squirrels (yes, squirrels cause a surprising number of power outages).

1.4.1 NERC CIP: North America's Smart Grid Bodyguards

Let's start with the big boss of North American energy security standards: NERC CIP (North American Electric Reliability Corporation Critical Infrastructure Protection). This set of standards applies to all power grid operators in the U.S., Canada, and parts of Mexico, and it's all about keeping cyber threats from knocking out critical infrastructure.

🔒 Why NERC CIP Exists:

In 2003, a massive blackout hit the U.S. and Canada, affecting 50 million people.

Investigators found a mix of system failures and poor security played a role.

The government said, "Alright, no more messing around," and NERC CIP was born.

🔑 Key NERC CIP Requirements:

CIP-002: Identify critical assets (because you can't protect what you don't know exists).

CIP-005: Secure electronic perimeters (firewalls, segmentation, access control).

CIP-007: Manage system security (patching, monitoring, and access logs).

CIP-010: Regularly test security controls (because compliance without enforcement is pointless).

💡 Why It Matters:

Failing a NERC CIP audit isn't just embarrassing—it's expensive. Fines can reach $1 million per day, per violation. That's enough to make any utility company take cybersecurity seriously.

1.4.2 IEC 62443: The Global Standard for Industrial Cybersecurity

Now, let's talk international. While NERC CIP is a heavyweight in North America, the IEC 62443 standard is used worldwide to secure industrial control systems (ICS), SCADA networks, and critical infrastructure.

🔒 Why IEC 62443 Exists:

Industrial systems were never designed for security—they were designed for reliability.

As more industrial devices get connected, cyberattacks have skyrocketed.

IEC 62443 helps bring security up to modern standards for industrial networks.

📍 Key IEC 62443 Components:

IEC 62443 breaks security down into four layers:

General requirements (risk assessments, security policies).

Policies for industrial system operators (protecting control systems).

Requirements for system integrators (securely designing infrastructure).

Requirements for device manufacturers (securing IoT devices from the start).

💡 Why It Matters:

IEC 62443 is flexible and scalable—it applies to utilities, smart grids, oil refineries, water treatment plants, and even manufacturing. If you're securing anything industrial that connects to a network, this is your go-to standard.

1.4.3 ISO 27019: Information Security for the Energy Sector

Finally, we have ISO 27019, the less famous sibling of the ISO 27000 family of cybersecurity standards. If NERC CIP is about grid security and IEC 62443 is about industrial security, ISO 27019 focuses on protecting sensitive energy data.

🔏 Why ISO 27019 Exists:

Energy companies store huge amounts of valuable data (billing info, grid configurations, customer details).

Hackers love stealing this data for fraud, extortion, and espionage.

ISO 27019 ensures confidentiality, integrity, and availability (CIA) of energy sector information.

📍 Key ISO 27019 Requirements:

Data encryption (protecting sensitive grid and customer data).

Access control (limiting who can see what).

Incident response plans (because sooner or later, something will go wrong).

💡 Why It Matters:

ISO 27019 helps utility companies and grid operators reduce the risk of data breaches and cyberattacks—essential in a world where ransomware attacks are increasing by 150% year over year.

Final Thoughts: Cybersecurity Compliance Is Not Optional

I get it—reading about compliance isn't as exciting as hacking into a smart meter, but these regulations exist for a reason. Without them, utility companies would cut corners, security would be an afterthought, and hackers would have a field day.

Think of NERC CIP, IEC 62443, and ISO 27019 as the cybersecurity rulebook for keeping the lights on and the bad guys out. Sure, compliance can be a headache, but the alternative is far worse—massive blackouts, skyrocketing ransomware attacks, and regulators knocking on your door with million-dollar fines.

So, whether you're a security professional, a grid operator, or just someone who enjoys having electricity, understanding these standards is crucial. Because in today's world, smart grids are only as smart as their cybersecurity. And trust me—you don't want to be the one explaining to the government why your power plant got hacked. 🔥💡💻

1.5 Ethical and Legal Considerations in Smart Grid Security Testing

Alright, let's talk about the rules of engagement—because hacking a smart grid for fun or without permission is a great way to meet the FBI (and not in a good way).

Look, I get it. Breaking into systems, testing vulnerabilities, and exposing security flaws is thrilling. But when it comes to critical infrastructure, one mistake can mean millions of people losing power—and that's before the lawsuits, fines, and potential prison time.

So, before you start scanning networks, exploiting firmware, or testing smart meter security, you need to understand the ethical and legal boundaries. Because in the world of smart grid cybersecurity, one wrong move can turn you from a hero into a headline.

1.5.1 The Ethics of Smart Grid Security Testing

Let's start with the moral side of things. Just because you can hack a system doesn't mean you should—especially when it comes to power grids, SCADA systems, and energy infrastructure. The goal of ethical hacking is to improve security, not cause chaos.

🥷 White Hat vs. Black Hat vs. Gray Hat

White Hat: You're a security professional hired to find vulnerabilities legally.

Black Hat: You're hacking for personal gain, causing disruption, or selling exploits.

Gray Hat: You find vulnerabilities without permission, then tell the company—but you still broke the law.

Even if your intentions are good, hacking a live smart grid without permission makes you a cybercriminal. Period.

🔑 Ethical Security Testing Guidelines:

Get explicit permission. No "I was just testing" excuses.

Follow responsible disclosure. Found a vulnerability? Report it the right way.

Minimize disruption. Testing should never take down the grid.

Know when to walk away. If you can't test something legally, don't.

1.5.2 The Legal Side: What You Can and Cannot Do

Now, let's talk about laws, because accidentally committing a felony isn't a great career move.

📖 Key Laws That Affect Smart Grid Hacking

1. Computer Fraud and Abuse Act (CFAA) – USA

Covers unauthorized access to protected computer systems (which includes smart grids).

Even probing a smart grid network without permission could violate CFAA.

Penalties range from fines to years in prison (and no, "I was just testing" isn't a valid defense).

2. NERC CIP Compliance – North America

Utility companies must follow NERC CIP security standards.

Security researchers must follow legal guidelines for penetration testing.

Unauthorized access or disruptions? Serious federal offenses.

3. GDPR & Data Privacy Laws – Europe & Beyond

If your testing involves customer data, privacy laws kick in.

Unauthorized access to smart meter data? Major legal consequences.

4. International Hacking Laws

Different countries, different rules. What's legal in one country might be illegal in another.

Example: Some places treat ethical hacking the same as cybercrime—so always know local laws.

1.5.3 Responsible Disclosure: Reporting Vulnerabilities the Right Way

Let's say you find a massive security flaw in a smart grid system. Do you:

A) Report it responsibly and help fix the problem?
B) Tweet it out and watch the chaos unfold?
C) Sell it on the dark web and retire early?

If you picked B or C, congratulations—you're now a cybercriminal.

🚨 How to Report Security Flaws Ethically

Contact the company first—give them a chance to fix it.

Use official channels—some organizations have bug bounty programs.

Avoid public disclosure—don't make vulnerabilities easy for attackers.

Document everything—if someone questions your motives, you'll have proof.

💰 Do Smart Grid Companies Pay for Vulnerability Reports?

Sometimes! Some energy companies offer bug bounties for security researchers. However, many don't—so before you start hacking away, check if they have a disclosure program.

1.5.4 What Happens If You Break the Rules?

Let's say you ignore everything I just said and go rogue, hacking a smart grid system without permission. What's the worst that could happen?

⚡ Real-World Consequences:

Arrest & Federal Charges – Yep, you're going to court.

Massive Fines – Companies don't like hackers messing with their grids.

Job Blacklist – No ethical cybersecurity job will hire you after a conviction.

National Security Scrutiny – Smart grids are critical infrastructure—governments take attacks very seriously.

🚨 Real Case: The Guy Who Thought He Was "Helping"

A security researcher once hacked a city's power system without permission, thinking he was doing them a favor. Instead of a thank you, he got federal charges and a lifetime cybersecurity job ban. Lesson? Don't be that guy.

Final Thoughts: Be a Smart Grid Hero, Not a Villain

Look, ethical hacking is awesome—but only if you follow the rules. If you want to test smart grid security, do it legally. Work with energy companies, follow responsible disclosure, and never test without permission.

Because at the end of the day, smart grids power the world. Messing with them isn't just a "cool hack"—it can cause blackouts, financial losses, and even put lives at risk. And trust me, you don't want to be the person responsible for that.

So go forth, be ethical, and hack smart—not illegal. 🚀

Chapter 2: Smart Grid Network Architecture and Communication Protocols

Ah, the beautiful chaos of smart grid communication! Imagine a room full of engineers arguing in different languages, but somehow, they still manage to keep the lights on. That's basically what's happening inside the power grid—except instead of people, it's machines yelling at each other using protocols like DNP3, Modbus, and IEC 61850. And guess what? Hackers love eavesdropping on these conversations. From wireless tech like Zigbee and LoRa to 5G-powered smart meters, each component of the grid has its own quirks, and trust me, some of them are about as secure as a diary with a flimsy lock.

Smart grid communication networks form the backbone of modern energy infrastructure, enabling real-time data exchange between power plants, substations, smart meters, and control centers. These networks rely on a mix of wired and wireless protocols, including SCADA, AMI, and EMS, each with specific security challenges. Understanding these protocols is crucial for identifying vulnerabilities and implementing protective measures. This chapter explores the key communication technologies used in the smart grid, their security implications, and best practices for securing network traffic against eavesdropping, tampering, and unauthorized access.

2.1 Overview of Smart Grid Communication Networks (AMI, SCADA, EMS)

Ah, the smart grid—where power meets cyber connectivity and hackers meet new opportunities (just kidding... mostly).

Once upon a time, power grids were simple: electricity flowed, meters spun, and nobody worried about cybersecurity because nothing was connected. Then, the world said, "Let's make everything smarter!"—and suddenly, our grids were full of IoT devices, real-time data, and attack surfaces as wide as Texas.

At the heart of this digital transformation are three key communication networks:

Advanced Metering Infrastructure (AMI) – The system that talks to your electric meter.

Supervisory Control and Data Acquisition (SCADA) – The system that controls the grid's backbone.

Energy Management Systems (EMS) – The brain that optimizes energy flow.

These networks are essential for efficiency, automation, and keeping the lights on—but they also introduce new vulnerabilities. If you're defending the smart grid (or thinking like an attacker), understanding how these networks communicate is step one.

2.1.1 Advanced Metering Infrastructure (AMI): The Smart Meter Network

Ever wonder how your power company knows exactly how much electricity you use—down to the hour—without sending someone to read the meter? That's AMI in action.

⚡ What is AMI?

AMI is the two-way communication system that connects smart meters to the grid. It enables remote monitoring, real-time billing, and even automatic outage detection.

🔗 How AMI Works:

Smart meters record electricity usage and send it to the utility company.

Data travels through wireless (RF, Wi-Fi, Zigbee, LoRa) or wired (PLC, fiber) networks.

Utilities analyze this data to manage demand, detect fraud, and optimize energy distribution.

🔒 Why AMI is a Security Risk:

Unencrypted meter traffic can be intercepted and manipulated.

Man-in-the-middle (MITM) attacks can alter billing data.

Remote disconnect commands could be exploited to turn off power.

🛡️ Securing AMI:

Encryption to protect data in transit.

Authentication to prevent unauthorized access.

Intrusion detection systems (IDS) to monitor anomalies.

2.1.2 Supervisory Control and Data Acquisition (SCADA): The Grid's Control System

If AMI is the ears and eyes of the smart grid, SCADA is the nervous system.

⚡ What is SCADA?

SCADA is used to monitor and control critical infrastructure, including power plants, substations, and transmission lines. It collects real-time data from sensors and sends commands to remote devices.

∞ How SCADA Works:

Field devices (RTUs, PLCs) collect sensor data (voltage, frequency, temperature).

Data flows to SCADA servers over private networks or VPNs.

Grid operators monitor and control power distribution remotely.

🔒 Why SCADA is a Security Risk:

Legacy protocols (Modbus, DNP3) were not designed with security in mind.

Weak authentication means attackers could hijack control commands.

Air-gapped systems aren't always air-gapped—modern SCADA connects to IT networks.

□□ Securing SCADA:

Network segmentation to isolate SCADA from corporate IT systems.

Multi-factor authentication (MFA) to prevent unauthorized access.

Security patches for outdated control systems.

2.1.3 Energy Management System (EMS): The Brain of the Smart Grid

While SCADA manages the physical flow of electricity, EMS manages the big picture—balancing supply and demand, predicting failures, and keeping the grid stable.

⚡ What is EMS?

EMS is a software platform that helps utility companies make real-time decisions. It integrates AI, machine learning, and predictive analytics to optimize energy distribution.

∞ How EMS Works:

Collects SCADA data and analyzes grid performance.

Predicts power demand fluctuations and adjusts generation accordingly.

Detects faults or inefficiencies and recommends corrective actions.

🔒 Why EMS is a Security Risk:

A compromised EMS can manipulate the entire power grid.

Cloud-based EMS solutions are susceptible to data breaches.

Insider threats (disgruntled employees) can cause intentional disruptions.

☐☐ Securing EMS:

Role-based access control (RBAC) to limit who can modify grid settings.

Data encryption to protect grid telemetry.

AI-driven anomaly detection to spot cyberattacks before they escalate.

Final Thoughts: The Smart Grid is Only as Smart as Its Security

The smart grid's communication networks are what make real-time power management possible—but they also create a massive attack surface. If you're in charge of securing it, you need to understand how AMI, SCADA, and EMS interact—and where attackers will try to break in.

Because let's face it: Hackers love grids. Whether it's nation-state cyber warfare or some teenager trying to lower their power bill, the threats are real.

So, the question isn't whether the grid will be attacked—it's when. And when that time comes, will we be ready?

2.2 Common Protocols: DNP3, Modbus, IEC 61850, MQTT, and OPC-UA

If smart grid communication networks are the nervous system of the grid, then protocols are the languages they speak. And let me tell you—some of these languages are so old, they make ancient Latin look modern.

Picture this: You've got thousands of power stations, substations, smart meters, and IoT devices all trying to communicate with each other—but they weren't all designed by the same manufacturer, and many of them were built decades ago, before cybersecurity was even a thing. The result? A messy, complicated web of communication protocols, some of which are about as secure as a diary with a broken lock.

But don't worry—by the end of this chapter, you'll know the key smart grid protocols (DNP3, Modbus, IEC 61850, MQTT, and OPC-UA) and their strengths, weaknesses, and security concerns.

2.2.1 DNP3: The Old-School Workhorse

⚡ What is DNP3?

The Distributed Network Protocol 3 (DNP3) is like that reliable, slightly outdated friend who still gets the job done. Originally developed in the 1990s, it's widely used in SCADA systems to enable communication between remote terminal units (RTUs), intelligent electronic devices (IEDs), and control centers.

∞ How DNP3 Works:

Uses a master-slave architecture—control centers issue commands, field devices respond.

Supports time-stamped data for event logging.

Can operate over serial, TCP/IP, or radio.

🔒 Why DNP3 is a Security Risk:

No native encryption—attackers can intercept and modify commands.

Man-in-the-middle (MITM) attacks can manipulate SCADA data.

Replay attacks allow hackers to resend old commands.

⬚⬚ Securing DNP3:

Use DNP3 Secure Authentication (DNP3-SA) for stronger authentication.

Deploy VPNs to encrypt communication.

Monitor traffic for anomalies (unexpected commands, repeated signals).

2.2.2 Modbus: The Granddaddy of Industrial Protocols

⚡ What is Modbus?

First introduced in 1979, Modbus is the oldest protocol on this list—and it shows. It's commonly used in industrial automation, SCADA, and smart grid systems to connect field devices with control systems.

∞ How Modbus Works:

Uses a client-server model (aka master-slave).

Supports both serial (Modbus RTU) and Ethernet (Modbus TCP).

Lightweight and simple, making it popular in legacy systems.

🔒 Why Modbus is a Security Risk:

No built-in authentication—anyone on the network can send commands.

No encryption—attackers can sniff or modify data.

Denial of Service (DoS) attacks can flood Modbus devices with requests.

□□ Securing Modbus:

Use firewalls to restrict Modbus traffic.

Implement access control lists (ACLs) to limit device access.

Transition to Modbus Secure (which adds TLS encryption).

2.2.3 IEC 61850: The Smart Grid's Universal Language

⚡ What is IEC 61850?

IEC 61850 is the modern, flexible protocol designed specifically for smart grid substations. Unlike DNP3 and Modbus, it's object-oriented, meaning devices don't just exchange raw numbers—they exchange meaningful, structured data.

🔗 How IEC 61850 Works:

Uses GOOSE (Generic Object-Oriented Substation Events) for fast, real-time messaging.

Supports peer-to-peer communication (no master-slave dependency).

Optimized for high-speed data exchange in substations.

🔒 Why IEC 61850 is a Security Risk:

GOOSE messages can be spoofed to send false substation commands.

Lack of authentication in early implementations.

Denial of Service (DoS) attacks can overload substation networks.

□□ Securing IEC 61850:

Enable message authentication for GOOSE traffic.

Use network segmentation to isolate substation communication.

Apply intrusion detection systems (IDS) to monitor suspicious activities.

2.2.4 MQTT: The Lightweight IoT Messenger

⚡ What is MQTT?

Message Queuing Telemetry Transport (MQTT) is the protocol of choice for IoT devices, including smart meters, sensors, and distributed energy resources (DERs). It's designed for low-bandwidth, high-latency networks—perfect for remote energy monitoring.

∞ How MQTT Works:

Uses a publish-subscribe model (instead of request-response).

Devices publish data to a broker, which forwards it to subscribers.

Supports QoS (Quality of Service) levels to ensure reliable message delivery.

🔒 Why MQTT is a Security Risk:

No default encryption—data can be intercepted.

Weak authentication means unauthorized devices can publish/subscribe.

Denial of Service (DoS) attacks can overload the broker.

🔲🔲 Securing MQTT:

Use TLS encryption to protect data in transit.

Implement strong authentication (e.g., username/password, certificates).

Monitor and restrict topics to prevent unauthorized data publishing.

2.2.5 OPC-UA: The Secure Industrial Standard

⚡ What is OPC-UA?

OPC-UA (Open Platform Communications – Unified Architecture) is the gold standard for industrial IoT (IIoT) security. It's designed for cross-platform interoperability while baking in security features from the start.

🔗 How OPC-UA Works:

Uses client-server and publish-subscribe models.

Supports encryption, authentication, and access control.

Enables seamless communication between IT and OT networks.

🔓 Why OPC-UA is a Security Risk:

Misconfigured security settings can leave it vulnerable.

Man-in-the-middle (MITM) attacks are possible if encryption isn't enabled.

Denial of Service (DoS) attacks can disrupt operations.

🛡️ Securing OPC-UA:

Always enable encryption and authentication.

Use role-based access control (RBAC) to limit privileges.

Monitor logs for suspicious activities.

Final Thoughts: Speak the Language, Secure the Grid

Smart grid protocols are the backbone of energy communication—but many were never designed with security in mind. From the legacy weaknesses of DNP3 and Modbus to the modern flexibility of IEC 61850, MQTT, and OPC-UA, understanding these protocols is crucial for both defenders and attackers.

So, the next time someone tells you, "The grid is secure", ask them:

Are you encrypting DNP3 traffic?

Is your MQTT broker protected?

Have you secured your OPC-UA implementation?

Because if the answer is "Uh… not really", well… I hope you like candlelight dinners, because a blackout might be coming soon.

2.3 Wireless and RF Technologies in Smart Grid (LoRa, Zigbee, 5G, Wi-SUN)

If wires are the veins of the smart grid, then wireless technologies are like telepathic superpowers—letting devices talk to each other without the hassle of physical connections. But just like superpowers, they come with their own risks: eavesdroppers, imposters, and interference attacks. Imagine trying to have a top-secret conversation in a room full of hackers with parabolic microphones—yeah, that's wireless security in a nutshell.

From low-power IoT protocols like LoRa and Zigbee to high-speed cellular networks like 5G and the mesh-based magic of Wi-SUN, wireless technologies are critical for smart grids, but also introduce serious attack surfaces. Let's break down what these technologies do, where they shine, and where they totally drop the ball when it comes to security.

2.3.1 LoRa: The Long-Distance Whisperer

⚡ What is LoRa?

LoRa (Long Range) is the quiet, energy-efficient workhorse of the smart grid, designed for long-range, low-power communication. It's commonly used for smart metering, grid monitoring, and remote energy sensors.

👓 How LoRa Works:

Operates on sub-GHz frequencies (typically 868 MHz in Europe, 915 MHz in the US).

Uses chirp spread spectrum modulation, making it resilient to interference.

Supports LoRaWAN, a network protocol for cloud-based device management.

🔒 Why LoRa is a Security Risk:

No built-in encryption in raw LoRa (LoRaWAN adds some security).

Replay attacks can be used to resend old data packets.

Jamming attacks can easily disrupt LoRa signals due to weak signal strength.

🔐 Securing LoRa:

Use LoRaWAN with AES-128 encryption.

Implement device authentication to prevent rogue nodes.

Monitor for signal anomalies to detect interference or jamming.

2.3.2 Zigbee: The Smart Grid's IoT Social Network

⚡ What is Zigbee?

Zigbee is like a hyperactive gossip network for IoT devices—quick, lightweight, and designed for short-range, low-power communication. It's commonly used in smart meters, energy management systems, and home automation.

∞ How Zigbee Works:

Uses IEEE 802.15.4 for short-range wireless communication.

Supports mesh networking, so devices relay messages to extend range.

Operates on 2.4 GHz, meaning it shares space with Wi-Fi and Bluetooth.

🔒 Why Zigbee is a Security Risk:

Weak default encryption keys in older implementations.

Easily jammed due to its low-power nature.

MITM (Man-in-the-Middle) attacks can intercept Zigbee traffic.

🔲 Securing Zigbee:

Use Zigbee 3.0, which improves encryption and authentication.

Change default network keys—seriously, don't use the manufacturer's default.

Monitor for rogue Zigbee devices trying to join the network.

2.3.3 5G: The Smart Grid's High-Speed Express Lane

⚡ What is 5G?

5G is the new shiny thing in wireless communications, boasting blazing speeds, ultra-low latency, and massive device connectivity—perfect for real-time smart grid control, EV charging, and distributed energy systems.

∞ How 5G Works:

Operates on multiple frequency bands (low, mid, and mmWave).

Supports massive IoT device connectivity (up to a million devices per square km).

Enables network slicing, allowing virtual networks tailored for smart grids.

🔒 Why 5G is a Security Risk:

New tech means new attack vectors—5G networks are still evolving.

Signaling attacks can be used to disrupt network services.

Supply chain risks—compromised hardware from certain vendors can create backdoors.

🔲 Securing 5G:

Use strong end-to-end encryption for smart grid data.

Monitor 5G signaling traffic for anomalies.

Work with trusted hardware vendors to reduce supply chain risks.

2.3.4 Wi-SUN: The Mesh Network Built for Smart Cities

⚡ What is Wi-SUN?

Wi-SUN (Wireless Smart Utility Network) is the rugged, self-healing network that's built specifically for smart grid infrastructure. Think of it as Zigbee on steroids, capable of covering entire cities with a low-power, high-resilience network.

∞ How Wi-SUN Works:

Uses IEEE 802.15.4g standard for industrial-grade mesh networking.

Supports self-healing networks, meaning nodes automatically reroute around failures.

Operates on sub-GHz frequencies, offering long-range connectivity.

🔒 Why Wi-SUN is a Security Risk:

If one node is compromised, it can spread to others in the mesh.

Wireless jamming can disrupt network stability.

Some implementations lack proper authentication, allowing rogue devices to join.

⬜⬜ Securing Wi-SUN:

Enable strong authentication and encryption (Wi-SUN FAN 1.0 has security features).

Regularly audit network nodes to detect compromised devices.

Use frequency-hopping techniques to reduce jamming risks.

Final Thoughts: Wireless is Powerful, But Also Dangerous

Wireless and RF technologies are critical for enabling smart grids, but let's be real—they're also prime targets for hackers. LoRa might be great for long-distance communication, but it's vulnerable to jamming. Zigbee makes home automation easy, but it's also easily spoofed. 5G promises lightning-fast connectivity, but it introduces new cyber risks. And Wi-SUN? Well, if you're not securing your mesh properly, you might as well invite attackers to the party.

So next time someone says, "We should go wireless!", ask them:

What security measures are in place?

Are you encrypting your data?

How will you handle jamming attacks?

Because if the answer is "Uhhh...", you might want to grab a Faraday cage and start preparing for some wireless mayhem.

2.4 Vulnerabilities in Smart Grid Communication Channels

Let's face it—communication is hard. Ever tried explaining Wi-Fi issues to your grandparents? Now imagine trying to secure an entire smart grid, where billions of devices are constantly talking to each other. It's like a never-ending group chat, except some participants are malicious hackers looking to eavesdrop, manipulate, or completely break the system.

From data interception and protocol weaknesses to man-in-the-middle attacks and jamming, smart grid communication channels are full of security holes just waiting to be exploited. Let's break them down and figure out how to plug these leaks before cybercriminals start running the show.

2.4.1 Eavesdropping and Data Interception

⚡ What's the Risk?

Imagine whispering a secret, but someone's got a hidden microphone. That's eavesdropping in the smart grid—a hacker intercepting unencrypted or weakly protected communications between devices, SCADA systems, and control centers.

☐☐ How Hackers Exploit It:

Sniffing unencrypted traffic in AMI (Advanced Metering Infrastructure) and SCADA networks.

Intercepting wireless transmissions in Zigbee, LoRa, and Wi-SUN networks.

Using MITM (Man-in-the-Middle) attacks to modify data before it reaches its destination.

□□ How to Defend Against It:

Encrypt all data transmissions (AES-256 for the win!).

Use VPNs and secure tunneling for sensitive network traffic.

Implement mutual authentication so devices verify who they're talking to.

2.4.2 Man-in-the-Middle (MITM) Attacks

⚡ What's the Risk?

A MITM attack is like a fake customer service rep rerouting your bank calls—except here, hackers intercept smart grid data, modify commands, or inject malicious responses.

□□ How Hackers Exploit It:

Rerouting smart meter data to manipulate billing.

Faking SCADA commands to disrupt grid operations.

Spoofing authentication tokens to gain control over devices.

□□ How to Defend Against It:

Use TLS (Transport Layer Security) for all smart grid communications.

Deploy digital signatures to ensure data integrity.

Enable intrusion detection systems to catch MITM attempts in real time.

2.4.3 Wireless Jamming and Denial of Service (DoS) Attacks

⚡ What's the Risk?

Jamming attacks are like blasting heavy metal at full volume in a library—legitimate signals get drowned out, making devices unable to communicate. If hackers jam wireless signals in a smart grid, critical operations can grind to a halt.

□□ **How Hackers Exploit It:**

Jamming Zigbee-based smart meters to disrupt billing.

Overloading LoRa networks with garbage data.

Flooding SCADA networks with excessive requests to cause a DoS attack.

□□ **How to Defend Against It:**

Use frequency-hopping spread spectrum (FHSS) to avoid static jamming.

Deploy redundant communication paths (Wi-SUN + cellular backup).

Monitor signal anomalies to detect jamming attempts.

2.4.4 Protocol Vulnerabilities in Smart Grid Networks

⚡ **What's the Risk?**

Not all smart grid protocols were built with security in mind. Some are old, outdated, or simply too trusting, making them prime targets for attackers.

□□ **How Hackers Exploit It:**

DNP3 (Distributed Network Protocol 3): Lacks encryption in older versions, making it vulnerable to spoofing.

Modbus: Originally designed for serial connections, it has no authentication, allowing unauthorized command execution.

MQTT (Message Queuing Telemetry Transport): If misconfigured, attackers can publish rogue commands to IoT devices.

□□ **How to Defend Against It:**

Upgrade to secure versions (DNP3 Secure Authentication, Modbus TLS, MQTT with authentication).

Segment networks to prevent protocol exploits from spreading.

Use access control lists (ACLs) to limit communication privileges.

2.4.5 Supply Chain Attacks on Communication Hardware

⚡ What's the Risk?

Imagine buying a brand-new router… only to find out it's got a backdoor installed by the manufacturer. That's a supply chain attack—compromising hardware or firmware before it even reaches the grid.

⬜⬜ How Hackers Exploit It:

Planting backdoors in communication modules before they're deployed.

Using counterfeit network equipment that contains hidden vulnerabilities.

Injecting malware into firmware updates for smart meters and control devices.

⬜⬜ How to Defend Against It:

Source equipment from trusted vendors.

Verify firmware integrity before deploying updates.

Implement hardware-based security (TPM chips, secure boot).

Final Thoughts: Plugging the Communication Leaks

Smart grids are only as secure as their communication channels. If you're transmitting critical energy data, you better encrypt it, authenticate it, and monitor it like your life depends on it—because in the case of the power grid, it literally might.

So next time someone says, "Wireless is secure enough", ask them:

Are you encrypting all data in transit?

Have you tested for jamming resistance?

Are your SCADA protocols actually secure?

If they blink twice and start sweating, you know there's work to be done.

2.5 Securing Smart Grid Protocols and Network Communications

Ever tried explaining to someone that Wi-Fi isn't just "the internet" but a network protocol? Now imagine that times a thousand—because in smart grids, we're dealing with SCADA, AMI, DNP3, Modbus, IEC 61850, MQTT, and a whole alphabet soup of protocols that power the entire energy sector. These protocols weren't always designed with security in mind, which means hackers see them as a buffet of vulnerabilities just waiting to be exploited.

So how do we secure smart grid communications and keep the bad guys from flipping the wrong switch? Buckle up, because we're about to dig into the best security practices, encryption strategies, and defensive mechanisms that will turn your smart grid into a fortress of cyber resilience.

2.5.1 The Golden Rule: Encrypt Everything

⚡ Why Encryption is Critical

If your communication isn't encrypted, you might as well be shouting grid commands into a hacker's microphone. Encryption ensures that even if an attacker intercepts data, they can't read or modify it without the correct keys.

⬜⬜ How to Implement Strong Encryption

TLS (Transport Layer Security): Secure web-based communications (MQTT, REST APIs, IEC 61850 over IP).

AES-256 (Advanced Encryption Standard): Encrypts sensitive grid data at rest and in transit.

IPsec (Internet Protocol Security): Protects IP-based smart grid traffic against tampering.

▶ Common Mistakes to Avoid

Using outdated encryption algorithms (DES, MD5, SHA-1 are hacker gold mines).

Hardcoding encryption keys in firmware (seriously, don't do this).

Forgetting key rotation, making it easier for attackers to crack long-term keys.

2.5.2 Authentication: Trust, But Verify

⚡ Why Authentication Matters

Imagine if anyone could walk into a power station and start pressing buttons. That's what weak authentication does—it lets unauthorized devices, users, or malware pretend to be legitimate and wreak havoc.

☐☐ Strong Authentication Methods

Mutual TLS (mTLS): Ensures that both client and server verify each other's identity.

PKI (Public Key Infrastructure): Provides secure, scalable authentication using certificates.

Multi-Factor Authentication (MFA): Adds an extra layer of security for remote grid operators.

▶ Common Mistakes to Avoid

Using default usernames/passwords (yes, people still do this).

Not revoking access for retired or compromised devices.

Relying on weak challenge-response mechanisms (e.g., legacy Modbus setups with no authentication).

2.5.3 Securing Smart Grid Protocols: Fixing the Weak Links

⚡ The Problem: Outdated and Vulnerable Protocols

Most legacy smart grid protocols were designed for efficiency, not security. DNP3, Modbus, and even some IEC 61850 implementations lack authentication, encryption, and integrity checks—making them hacker-friendly.

☐☐ How to Secure Key Smart Grid Protocols

◆ DNP3 (Distributed Network Protocol 3)

- **Weakness**: Older versions have no built-in encryption.
- **Solution**: Upgrade to DNP3 Secure Authentication (SA), which adds HMAC-based integrity checks and TLS support.

◆ Modbus (Used in ICS and SCADA)

- **Weakness**: No authentication or encryption by default.
- **Solution**: Use Modbus-TLS, implement firewall-based whitelisting, and disable unnecessary function codes.

◆ IEC 61850 (Power Grid Automation Protocol)

- **Weakness**: Some implementations don't enforce authentication.
- **Solution**: Enable Role-Based Access Control (RBAC) and ensure secure GOOSE (Generic Object-Oriented Substation Event) messaging.

◆ MQTT (Message Queue Telemetry Transport)

- **Weakness**: Misconfigured brokers allow unauthenticated connections.
- **Solution**: Require client certificates, enforce access control lists (ACLs), and use end-to-end encryption.

2.5.4 Network Segmentation: Keep the Bad Guys Contained

⚡ Why You Should Never Put Everything on One Network

If your smart meters, SCADA systems, and corporate IT share the same network, you've just made a hacker's life way too easy. Network segmentation ensures that if an attacker breaches one system, they can't hop into critical grid infrastructure.

☐☐ How to Segment Smart Grid Networks

Use VLANs (Virtual LANs): Separate smart meters, SCADA, and IT systems.

Implement Firewalls & Intrusion Detection Systems (IDS): Block unauthorized cross-network traffic.

Zero Trust Architecture: Assume no device is trustworthy by default and require strict access controls.

⚑ Common Mistakes to Avoid

Using flat networks with no segmentation.

Forgetting to monitor internal network traffic (insider threats are real).

Relying solely on perimeter firewalls—attackers can already be inside.

2.5.5 Monitoring and Anomaly Detection: Catching Attacks Before They Happen

⚡ Why Real-Time Monitoring is a Game-Changer

Hackers don't always announce themselves. Instead, they probe networks, test vulnerabilities, and exfiltrate data slowly. If you're not watching for unusual behavior, you'll only notice an attack when the lights go out.

☐☐ Smart Grid Security Monitoring Best Practices

Deploy SIEM (Security Information and Event Management) systems to log and analyze network activity.

Use AI-based anomaly detection to catch zero-day attacks.

Monitor OT (Operational Technology) and IT traffic separately—different threats target each.

⚑ Common Mistakes to Avoid

Ignoring failed authentication attempts (that could be brute-force attacks).

Not analyzing command logs—attackers often send test commands before launching full-scale attacks.

Thinking monitoring is a "set it and forget it" solution (it needs constant tuning).

Final Thoughts: You Can't Just Hope for Security—You Have to Build It

Smart grid communication security isn't optional. If you're transmitting power grid commands, you better encrypt them, authenticate them, and make sure no unauthorized device is in the mix. Otherwise, you're handing hackers the keys to the entire electrical infrastructure—and trust me, they won't just dim the lights for fun.

So next time someone says, "We don't need all this encryption and security nonsense", ask them:

What happens if someone hijacks our SCADA system?

How do we stop a rogue MQTT device from sending false data?

Are we sure no one's listening in on our power grid commands?

If the response is nervous laughter, it's time to start implementing real security measures—before the next blackout isn't an accident.

Chapter 3: Reconnaissance and Attack Surface Mapping

You know that old saying, "Know thy enemy"? Well, hackers take that very seriously. Before launching an attack, they do their homework—scouring the internet, poking at networks, and gathering juicy intel about smart meters, substations, and control systems. Tools like Shodan and Censys turn cyberspace into a hacker's playground, making it ridiculously easy to find internet-exposed energy infrastructure. And if that wasn't scary enough, passive and active network scanning can uncover even more secrets, making power companies look like they're playing cybersecurity on "easy mode."

Reconnaissance is the first step in a cyberattack, allowing adversaries to identify vulnerabilities before exploiting them. Attack surface mapping involves analyzing publicly available information, scanning networks for exposed assets, and fingerprinting devices to assess potential entry points. This chapter covers the methodologies used for reconnaissance in smart grid environments, including OSINT techniques, passive monitoring, and active scanning tools. It also provides guidelines for hardening smart grid systems against unauthorized discovery and limiting the exposure of critical infrastructure.

3.1 Identifying Critical Smart Grid Components and Devices

Ah, the smart grid—a futuristic, highly connected, and totally secure system, right? Well... not quite. While utilities love to brag about efficiency, automation, and real-time analytics, cybercriminals see something else entirely: a massive, juicy attack surface with countless entry points.

But before we can talk about hacking (or, you know, defending) the smart grid, we need to know what's inside this beast. What are the most critical components? Which devices are the biggest security risks? And most importantly, where should defenders focus their efforts? Let's break it all down.

3.1.1 The Smart Grid's Nervous System: Key Components

Think of the smart grid as a gigantic cyber-physical organism—a Frankenstein's monster of IT, OT (Operational Technology), IoT, and traditional power infrastructure. Every part plays a role in keeping the electricity flowing, but some components are way more critical than others.

⬜⬜ The Big Players in Smart Grid Infrastructure

1. Advanced Metering Infrastructure (AMI)

What it does: Collects and transmits electricity consumption data from smart meters to utilities.

Why it matters: It's the direct connection between utilities and millions of customers.

Security risk: Hackers can manipulate billing data, shut off meters, or even cause widespread outages.

2. Supervisory Control and Data Acquisition (SCADA) Systems

What it does: Monitors and controls power generation, transmission, and distribution.

Why it matters: It's basically the brain of the smart grid.

Security risk: A compromised SCADA system could mean nationwide blackouts (looking at you, Stuxnet and Industroyer).

3. Energy Management Systems (EMS)

What it does: Balances electricity supply and demand in real-time.

Why it matters: Helps prevent grid instability and cascading failures.

Security risk: Attackers could manipulate power flow and cause blackouts or equipment failures.

4. Distribution Management Systems (DMS)

What it does: Manages and automates power distribution.

Why it matters: It helps detect and respond to faults faster.

Security risk: Attackers could misdirect power flow, causing overloads or outages.

5. Remote Terminal Units (RTUs) & Programmable Logic Controllers (PLCs)

What they do: Act as the hands and feet of SCADA systems—remotely controlling substations, circuit breakers, and transformers.

Why they matter: These devices execute real-world power grid operations.

Security risk: If compromised, attackers can physically damage grid equipment.

6. Grid Edge Devices (DERs, Microgrids, and IoT Sensors)

What they do: Manage decentralized energy sources like solar panels, wind farms, and battery storage.

Why they matter: They enable clean energy integration and grid resilience.

Security risk: Poorly secured edge devices can be hijacked for DDoS attacks or manipulated to disrupt the grid.

7. Communication Networks and Protocols

What they do: Enable data exchange between all smart grid components.

Why they matter: The grid doesn't function without them.

Security risk: Weak encryption, unauthenticated devices, or legacy protocols can be exploited.

3.1.2 Identifying Critical Devices for Cybersecurity

Alright, now that we know the major players, let's talk about how to identify the most vulnerable targets. Attackers don't just randomly pick a device—they strategically choose their entry points based on vulnerabilities, network exposure, and potential impact.

📌 High-Risk Devices in Smart Grids

When securing a smart grid, prioritize the following:

1. Internet-Exposed Smart Grid Devices

- **Example**: Misconfigured SCADA systems, unpatched smart meters, or exposed EMS interfaces.
- **Why they're risky**: If Shodan or Censys can find them, so can attackers.

2. Legacy Systems with No Security Features

- **Example**: Older DNP3, Modbus, or proprietary industrial protocols with zero authentication.
- **Why they're risky:** These systems were built before cyberattacks were even a concern.

3. Remote Access Systems & VPN Gateways

- **Example**: Third-party vendor access to substations or power plants.
- **Why they're risky**: Weak credentials or phishing attacks on contractors can give hackers full grid access.

4. Edge IoT Devices with Weak Authentication

- **Example**: Smart sensors, DER controllers, or inverters in solar farms.
- **Why they're risky**: These devices often use default passwords and insecure firmware.

5. RF and Wireless Communication Systems

- **Example**: Zigbee-based smart meters, Wi-SUN-enabled substations, or LoRa-based IoT sensors.
- **Why they're risky:** Attackers can use RF sniffing, jamming, or replay attacks to disrupt communications.

3.1.3 How to Identify and Protect Critical Smart Grid Assets

🔍 Asset Discovery & Risk Assessment

Before you can protect something, you need to know it exists. Here's how to identify and secure critical smart grid assets:

1. Network Mapping & Inventory Management

Use Nmap, Nessus, or OpenVAS to scan and map all connected devices.

Implement asset tagging to categorize devices by risk level.

2. Vulnerability Scanning & Penetration Testing

Conduct regular penetration tests on smart meters, SCADA systems, and IoT sensors.

Identify default credentials, unpatched firmware, or exposed admin interfaces.

3. Implement Zero Trust Security

Enforce least privilege access—not every device needs full network visibility.

Use network segmentation to isolate critical systems from IoT devices.

4. Continuous Monitoring & Threat Detection

Deploy Intrusion Detection Systems (IDS) like Snort, Suricata, or Zeek.

Use AI-driven anomaly detection to spot unusual grid behavior.

Final Thoughts: You Can't Secure What You Don't See

Look, the smart grid is basically a giant cyber-physical playground for both engineers and hackers. If we don't know what devices are connected, where they are, and how they communicate, we're flying blind in a storm of cyber threats.

So next time someone says, "Our grid is totally secure", ask them:

Can you list every internet-facing smart meter?

Are your SCADA systems still running default passwords?

How many outdated RTUs are connected to your network?

If the answer is silence, nervous laughter, or "Uh… let me check", then congratulations! You just found your first cybersecurity risk. Now go secure that grid before someone else does it for you. 🚀

3.2 Using Shodan, Censys, and Open-Source Intelligence (OSINT) for Reconnaissance

Ever wondered how hackers magically find vulnerable systems on the internet? Do they have some super-secret spy satellite? A cyber crystal ball? Nope. They just use Shodan, Censys, and OSINT tools—which, fun fact, are freely available to anyone with an internet connection (yes, even your grandma).

In the world of smart grid cybersecurity, reconnaissance is the first step in an attack—and the first step in defending against one. If you know how attackers gather intelligence, you can spot and eliminate vulnerabilities before they do. So, let's dive into the art of finding exposed smart grid devices before the bad guys do.

3.2.1 What is OSINT and Why Does it Matter?

🔍 OSINT: The Hacker's Best Friend (and Yours, Too!)

Open-Source Intelligence (OSINT) is publicly available information that can be gathered from the internet. Think of it as cyber-stalking for cybersecurity—except instead of spying on your ex, you're looking for exposed smart meters, SCADA systems, and IoT devices.

Why OSINT is Critical for Smart Grid Security

Attackers use it to find vulnerable targets—before they even touch your network.

Defenders use it to identify security gaps—before attackers exploit them.

It requires zero hacking skills—just a search engine and a little curiosity.

So, let's talk about the most powerful OSINT tools that can help uncover security risks in smart grid infrastructure.

3.2.2 Shodan: The Search Engine for Hackers (and Security Pros)

🔲 What is Shodan?

Shodan is like Google, but instead of finding cat videos, it finds internet-connected devices—including SCADA systems, smart meters, power substations, and more.

How Shodan Works

It scans the internet 24/7, indexing any device with an open port.

It displays metadata, including IP addresses, open ports, protocols, and device banners.

It helps attackers and defenders find exposed and vulnerable systems.

Finding Exposed Smart Grid Devices with Shodan

Try searching for:

SCADA → Finds SCADA systems exposed online (terrifying).

port:502 modbus → Finds Modbus-based industrial controllers.

port:47808 bacnet → Exposes building automation systems.

port:20000 dnp3 → Reveals DNP3-controlled power grid devices.

Real-World Example:

In 2020, security researchers found thousands of SCADA and ICS devices on Shodan—many with default passwords or no authentication. Attackers could literally shut down parts of the power grid from their laptop. Yikes.

How to Defend Against Shodan Exposure

Block unnecessary ports (especially anything internet-facing).

Disable default credentials on SCADA/ICS devices.

Use VPNs and firewalls to hide critical systems.

Regularly check Shodan for your own assets (yes, really).

3.2.3 Censys: Like Shodan, But More Advanced

⬜ What is Censys?

Censys is another internet-wide scanning tool, but it's more detailed than Shodan. Think of it as Shodan's nerdy older brother—it provides deep insights into SSL/TLS configurations, certificates, and protocol details.

What Makes Censys Different?

It provides more structured, detailed reports.

It scans for SSL/TLS misconfigurations, which is critical for smart grid security.

It's often used by security researchers to track ICS device exposures.

Using Censys for Smart Grid Security

Search queries like:

services.service_name: "modbus" → Finds exposed Modbus devices.

services.http.response_body: "SCADA" → Identifies SCADA control panels.

parsed.names: "energy-company.com" → Finds all internet-facing devices for an energy company.

How to Defend Against Censys Scans

Use strong TLS configurations to avoid certificate leaks.

Monitor for exposed smart grid devices regularly.

Restrict access to SCADA interfaces with IP whitelisting.

3.2.4 Other OSINT Tools for Smart Grid Reconnaissance

🔍 Other Ways Attackers Gather Smart Grid Intelligence

1. Google Dorking (Hacking with Google)

Google can find sensitive smart grid information—if you know the right tricks. Try:

intitle:"SCADA Login" → Finds exposed SCADA login pages.

filetype:pdf "Smart Grid Security Policy" → Finds internal security documents.

inurl:/admin intitle:login → Finds admin panels for smart grid devices.

Defense:

Use "robots.txt" to prevent sensitive pages from being indexed.

Enforce authentication on all smart grid portals.

Regularly audit publicly exposed documents.

2. GitHub & Pastebin: The Accidental Data Leaks

Developers sometimes accidentally upload passwords, API keys, or system configs to GitHub. Attackers use:

site:github.com "password" → Finds hardcoded passwords.

site:pastebin.com "confidential" → Finds leaked smart grid configs.

Defense:

Use automated scanning tools like TruffleHog to detect secrets in code.

Enforce strict data policies for employees.

3.2.5 Final Thoughts: Beat Hackers at Their Own Game

Most cyberattacks don't start with some elite hacker breaking into systems—they start with publicly available data. If your smart meters, SCADA systems, or EMS dashboards are exposed on Shodan or Censys, congratulations—you've just made an attacker's job a whole lot easier.

So, what's the lesson here? Start thinking like an attacker:

✅ Run Shodan and Censys scans on your own network—before someone else does.

✅ Use Google Dorking to find your own leaks—before hackers do.

✅ Monitor OSINT sources for data breaches—because attackers definitely are.

And most importantly—secure your smart grid before it becomes an attacker's playground. 🚀

3.3 Passive and Active Network Scanning in Smart Grid Environments

Ah, network scanning—the cybersecurity equivalent of "peeking behind the curtain." If done right, you'll uncover a goldmine of information about smart grid devices, connections, and vulnerabilities. Done wrong? Well, you might accidentally trip an intrusion detection system, alert every SOC analyst in the building, or even crash a fragile industrial control system. (Oops.)

Before we go full hacker-mode, let's break it down: Passive scanning is the "stealthy spy" approach, and active scanning is more like banging on doors to see who answers. In the world of smart grid security, both methods are crucial for finding weak spots—before the bad guys do.

3.3.1 Understanding Passive and Active Scanning

🕵️ Passive Scanning: Sneaky, Silent, and Safe

Passive scanning is all about listening rather than probing. It's like sitting in a coffee shop with a newspaper, eavesdropping on conversations. In smart grid environments, passive scanning is preferred because it doesn't interfere with live systems—which is especially important when dealing with sensitive infrastructure like power grids, substations, and SCADA networks.

How Passive Scanning Works:

Sniffing network traffic without direct interaction.

Identifying devices, protocols, and data flows without triggering alarms.

Detecting anomalies, rogue devices, or unauthorized connections.

Common Passive Scanning Tools:

Wireshark – The Swiss Army knife of network sniffing.

Zeek (formerly Bro) – Monitors and analyzes live network traffic.

Passive Vulnerability Scanner (PVS) – A non-intrusive way to detect risks.

Passive Scanning in Smart Grids: What Can You Find?

Unencrypted SCADA traffic flowing over the network.

Unknown devices communicating with critical infrastructure.

Default or weak credentials being sent in plaintext.

Since passive scanning doesn't actively interact with devices, it's great for ongoing monitoring and reconnaissance—without risking system crashes or detection.

🔦 Active Scanning: Probing for Weaknesses

Active scanning is the loud and aggressive approach. Unlike passive scanning, this method directly interacts with devices, sending packets to see who's awake, what ports are open, and where the vulnerabilities are hiding.

It's riskier because some smart grid components—especially older industrial control systems—aren't built to handle direct probing. Scanning too aggressively can cause systems to crash, freeze, or even malfunction (which would make you really unpopular with grid operators).

How Active Scanning Works:

Sends requests to devices to identify active hosts, services, and vulnerabilities.

Maps the network topology to see how different components interact.

Finds misconfigurations, exposed ports, and weak authentication setups.

Common Active Scanning Tools:

Nmap – The gold standard for network reconnaissance.

Masscan – A ridiculously fast port scanner for large networks.

Zmap – Efficiently scans the entire internet (or at least a smart grid segment).

Metasploit – Automates vulnerability detection and exploitation.

Active Scanning in Smart Grids: What Can You Find?

Exposed ICS/SCADA devices with weak or no authentication.

Misconfigured firewalls allowing unauthorized access.

Vulnerable communication protocols (like DNP3, Modbus, or MQTT).

3.3.2 Risks of Active Scanning in Smart Grid Environments

⚠️ Why You Shouldn't Just Scan Everything Blindly

Smart grid systems aren't your typical IT network. They include legacy ICS devices, embedded sensors, and critical infrastructure that wasn't designed with cybersecurity in mind. Scanning these systems too aggressively can cause:

Service disruptions – Some ICS devices may reboot or crash when scanned.

False alarms – Security monitoring tools might detect scans as cyberattacks.

Regulatory violations – Unauthorized scanning of smart grid components could break compliance laws (oops).

To avoid accidentally causing a blackout while scanning a power grid, always:

✅ **Get permission first** – Unauthorized scanning can get you fired (or arrested).
✅ **Use controlled environments** – Test on a sandboxed or mirrored network.

✅ **Start with passive scanning** – Identify what's there before poking at it.

3.3.3 Combining Passive and Active Scanning for Smart Grid Security

☐ The Hybrid Approach: Best of Both Worlds

The best security strategy isn't choosing one method—it's combining both.

1☐ Start with Passive Scanning

Collect network data without disturbing live systems.

Identify normal vs. abnormal communication patterns.

Map out devices and protocols in use.

2☐ Move to Controlled Active Scanning

Only scan non-critical systems first.

Use slow and non-intrusive scans to avoid disruptions.

Prioritize low-risk devices before escalating to ICS/SCADA components.

3☐ Analyze and Act on Findings

Close unnecessary open ports.

Secure communication channels (e.g., encrypt DNP3, Modbus traffic).

Restrict unauthorized access to smart grid systems.

3.3.4 Final Thoughts: Scan Smart, Not Hard

Reconnaissance is the first step in hacking—and in defending. Whether you're an ethical hacker (yay, good guy) or a security pro defending a smart grid (also yay, good guy), knowing how to scan safely and effectively is crucial.

✅ Passive scanning keeps you stealthy and safe—great for ongoing monitoring.

✓ Active scanning is more powerful but riskier—use it wisely.

✓ A hybrid approach gives you the best security visibility.

And most importantly—if you're scanning a live smart grid, make sure you don't accidentally take down the power for an entire city. (Because explaining that to your boss would be… awkward.)

3.4 Firmware and Device Fingerprinting for Vulnerability Analysis

Ah, firmware—the soul of every smart grid device. It's like the operating system of embedded systems, quietly running everything from smart meters to SCADA controllers. And yet, it's often neglected in security audits, left outdated, unpatched, and wide open to cyberattacks.

If firmware is the brain of a device, fingerprinting is like reading its mind—without asking permission. It's a hacker's way of figuring out what's running under the hood, what vulnerabilities it has, and how to exploit them. But don't worry, we're on the good side (right?). So, let's crack open some firmware and uncover its secrets—without breaking the grid.

3.4.1 What is Firmware Fingerprinting?

Firmware fingerprinting is the process of identifying a device's firmware version, architecture, and configuration to determine potential vulnerabilities. Unlike traditional network scanning, which focuses on IP addresses and open ports, firmware fingerprinting digs deeper, analyzing the actual software and embedded code running on smart grid devices.

☐☐ **Why is Firmware Fingerprinting Important?**

Helps attackers identify outdated, vulnerable firmware versions.

Reveals hidden backdoors, weak cryptographic implementations, and debug interfaces.

Aids defenders in understanding and securing devices before an attacker exploits them.

Common Targets for Firmware Fingerprinting in Smart Grids

Smart meters – Often use custom or modified Linux-based firmware.

SCADA controllers & RTUs – Run proprietary firmware with hardcoded credentials.

IoT gateways & edge devices – May have unpatched security flaws.

Industrial routers & firewalls – Often ship with default admin passwords (which nobody ever changes □).

Firmware fingerprinting is the first step in vulnerability analysis, helping both attackers and defenders understand where the weaknesses lie before attempting exploitation or mitigation.

3.4.2 Methods for Firmware Fingerprinting

There are multiple ways to identify and extract firmware information—some more aggressive than others. Let's break them down:

1□ Passive Firmware Fingerprinting (Low Risk)

This method involves observing network traffic and device responses without actively interacting with them. Think of it as watching a device from a distance, taking notes, and waiting for it to reveal its secrets.

How it Works:

Capturing HTTP headers, SNMP responses, and device banners.

Monitoring firmware update requests sent over the network.

Analyzing protocol-specific responses (e.g., Modbus, DNP3, IEC 61850).

Tools for Passive Firmware Fingerprinting:

Shodan & Censys – Search exposed smart grid devices on the internet.

Wireshark – Capture firmware update packets in transit.

Bro/Zeek – Passively analyze industrial network traffic.

What You Can Find:

Firmware version numbers leaked in network packets.

Hardcoded API keys embedded in IoT communication traffic.

Unencrypted firmware updates downloaded in plain text.

The beauty of passive fingerprinting? It won't trigger alarms or crash fragile ICS devices. But if passive methods don't give you enough intel, it's time for a more hands-on approach…

2️ Active Firmware Fingerprinting (Higher Risk)

Active fingerprinting involves directly interacting with the device to extract firmware information. It's riskier but provides deeper insights into how a device operates.

How it Works:

Sending crafted requests to devices and analyzing responses.

Exploiting known vulnerabilities to extract firmware details.

Leveraging debug interfaces like JTAG, UART, and SPI.

Tools for Active Firmware Fingerprinting:

Nmap with NSE scripts – Scans devices and identifies firmware versions.

Binwalk – Extracts and analyzes firmware binaries.

JTAGulator & Bus Pirate – Dumps firmware via hardware debugging interfaces.

What You Can Find:

Default admin credentials hardcoded in firmware.

Debugging functions left enabled in production devices.

Hidden SSH or Telnet backdoors for remote access.

Active fingerprinting is powerful but dangerous—some ICS/SCADA devices are so fragile that aggressive scanning can crash them. So, unless you want to explain why half the power grid just went offline, proceed with extreme caution.

3.4.3 Extracting and Analyzing Firmware for Vulnerabilities

Once you've identified the firmware version, the next step is extracting and analyzing it for security flaws. This is where things get fun—because manufacturers often leave a trail of breadcrumbs leading to major security issues.

How to Extract Firmware

Downloading firmware updates from the vendor's website (easy mode).

Dumping firmware from the device's memory via JTAG, SPI, or UART.

Intercepting firmware updates over the network (if they aren't encrypted).

Analyzing Firmware for Security Flaws

Binwalk – Extracts firmware images and detects compressed file systems.

Firmwalker – Searches for passwords, SSH keys, and API tokens.

Ghidra/IDA Pro – Reverse engineers compiled firmware binaries.

Radare2 – A powerful open-source reverse engineering tool.

Common Firmware Vulnerabilities Found in Smart Grid Devices

✓ **Hardcoded credentials** – Default usernames and passwords embedded in firmware.
✓ **Unpatched security flaws** – Devices running outdated versions with known exploits.
✓ **Exposed debug interfaces** – UART, JTAG, and SPI interfaces left enabled.
✓ **Weak encryption or no encryption** – Firmware updates transmitted in plaintext.
✓ **Hidden backdoors** – Manufacturer-implemented remote access points.

Once vulnerabilities are found, attackers can craft exploits—while defenders can push firmware updates and harden security before disaster strikes.

3.4.4 Securing Smart Grid Firmware Against Cyber Threats

Now that we know how firmware can be fingerprinted and exploited, how do we protect it? Here's how:

1️⃣ Secure Firmware Updates

- Implement digital signatures to prevent tampering.
- Use encrypted update channels (no more plain HTTP downloads, please).
- Enforce firmware version control—no rolling back to vulnerable versions.

2️⃣ Disable Unnecessary Debug Interfaces

- Lock down JTAG, UART, and SPI to prevent unauthorized access.
- Require authentication for maintenance functions.

3️⃣ Regular Firmware Audits & Penetration Testing

- Scan for hardcoded credentials before deployment.
- Perform static and dynamic analysis on all firmware releases.
- Monitor for unauthorized firmware modifications.

3.4.5 Final Thoughts: Firmware is the Weakest Link—Secure It!

Smart grid security isn't just about protecting networks—it's also about locking down the very software running on critical infrastructure. Firmware is often ignored, but for hackers, it's an open invitation to wreak havoc.

✅ Fingerprinting helps identify weaknesses before attackers do.

✅ Analyzing firmware exposes security gaps manufacturers miss.

✅ Securing firmware ensures the grid stays resilient against cyber threats.

And remember—if your firmware is outdated and insecure, your entire smart grid is one firmware update away from disaster. So, secure it before someone else does… the wrong way. 😺

3.5 Hardening Smart Grid Systems Against Unauthorized Discovery

You know what's fun? Not getting hacked. Unfortunately, many smart grid operators seem to think "security through obscurity" is a winning strategy. Spoiler alert: it isn't.

Hackers, pentesters, and nation-state actors are always on the hunt for exposed smart grid infrastructure. Using tools like Shodan, Censys, and OSINT techniques, they can map out critical components without ever touching the network—like a digital ninja casing a joint before a heist. The goal of this chapter? Make sure your smart grid doesn't show up on their radar.

3.5.1 The Danger of Unauthorized Discovery

Before we dive into defenses, let's get one thing straight: discovery is the first step in every cyberattack. If attackers can't find your systems, they can't hack them.

Here's how unauthorized discovery can lead to disaster:

🔲🔲 **What Attackers Can Find:**

Exposed Smart Grid Devices – RTUs, SCADA systems, smart meters, and gateways.

Firmware & Software Versions – Outdated, unpatched, and vulnerable to known exploits.

Misconfigured Services – Open ports, weak authentication, and default credentials.

Hidden Debug Interfaces – JTAG, UART, Telnet, or SSH backdoors.

🔦 **Why It's Dangerous:**

Attackers don't even need to scan your network. Public-facing devices can be found with a simple Google search.

A single exposed device can lead to full network compromise.

Regulatory fines and legal trouble if critical systems aren't properly secured.

The good news? We can make discovery much harder for attackers. Let's explore how.

3.5.2 Locking Down Public Exposure (OSINT Defense)

The first step in hardening your smart grid is reducing its digital footprint. If your devices show up on Shodan, Censys, or Google Dorks, that's strike one.

✅ **How to Reduce Public Exposure:**

◆ **Scan Yourself First** – Use Shodan, Censys, and FOFA to check if your smart grid infrastructure is exposed.
◆ **Remove Unnecessary Public IPs** – Critical systems should be isolated from the internet.
◆ **Disable Service Banners** – Attackers love when your devices proudly announce their firmware version.
◆ **Harden Cloud-Based SCADA/EMS** – If you're using cloud services, make sure authentication and encryption are airtight.

☐ **Tools to Use:**

Shodan & Censys – Find publicly exposed devices.

Google Dorking – Search for misconfigured or indexed smart grid components.

Attack Surface Management (ASM) Tools – Use tools like SurfaceBrowser, Assetnote, or SecurityTrails to monitor exposure.

A well-secured smart grid should be invisible to external discovery. If it can't be found, it can't be attacked.

3.5.3 Network Segmentation & Firewall Strategies
Even if attackers do find your devices, the next layer of defense is network segmentation—because not every system should be able to talk to every other system.

🔒 Best Practices for Network Segmentation:

✅ **Separate IT & OT Networks** – Your SCADA network should not be accessible from corporate or external networks.

✅ **Implement VLANs & Subnetting** – Keep AMI, SCADA, and EMS systems isolated.

✅ **Use Air Gaps Where Possible** – Critical infrastructure should never be directly connected to the internet.

✅ **Strict Firewall Rules** – Only allow whitelisted IPs and services to communicate.

🔥 Firewalls: Your First Line of Defense

Block all inbound traffic by default—only allow what's necessary.

Monitor and log all attempted access—early detection saves lives.

Apply deep packet inspection (DPI)—especially for Modbus, DNP3, and IEC 61850 traffic.

A well-segmented network makes it significantly harder for an attacker to move laterally—even if they breach one system, they won't be able to access everything else.

3.5.4 Preventing Passive & Active Scanning

Attackers love scanning networks—it's how they find weaknesses. Let's make that job as painful as possible for them.

🔲🔲 Passive Discovery (How Attackers See You Without Scanning)

Hackers don't always need to send probes; they can just listen to the network. Some key passive discovery methods include:

Packet Sniffing – Capturing unencrypted data with tools like Wireshark.

Analyzing Broadcast Traffic – Devices that send broadcast or multicast messages reveal valuable info.

Intercepting Firmware Updates – If updates are sent unencrypted, attackers can extract version details and vulnerabilities.

🚀 How to Defend:

✓ **Encrypt All Communications** – No plaintext protocols. Period.
✓ **Disable Unnecessary Broadcasts** – Reduce network noise.
✓ **Implement MAC Address Filtering** – Only allow authorized devices.

✳ Active Discovery (How Attackers Probe Your Network)

More aggressive attackers will actively scan your infrastructure to look for open ports and vulnerabilities. They use:

Nmap & Masscan – Quick scans to find open services.

Modbus/DNP3 Probing – Interacting with ICS/SCADA protocols.

Firmware Exploits – If they know your firmware version, they might already have an exploit ready.

☐ How to Defend:

✓ **Use Intrusion Detection Systems (IDS)** – Tools like Zeek/Bro or Snort can detect scans.
✓ **Rate-Limit Network Requests** – Slow down aggressive scanning.
✓ **Deception Tactics (Honeypots)** – Waste attackers' time by feeding them fake data.

If you make scanning painful, most attackers will move on to an easier target.

3.5.5 Deception Strategies: Hide in Plain Sight

Want to really mess with attackers? Use deception tactics. Make them waste time, effort, and resources chasing ghosts.

🎭 Best Deception Techniques:

Deploy ICS Honeypots – Use Conpot or GridPot to lure attackers into fake systems.

Fake Service Banners – Instead of revealing real versions, respond with misleading data.

Randomized MAC Addresses – Prevent passive fingerprinting.

Adaptive Network Defenses – Automatically change port numbers, IP addresses, and routes to confuse attackers.

Deception doesn't stop attacks, but it slows them down and makes hacking much harder.

Final Thoughts: Make Hackers Work for It!

Hardening your smart grid against discovery isn't just about hiding—it's about making everything more difficult for attackers. If they can't find your systems, they can't exploit them. And if they do find them? Make their life hell.

- **Remove public exposure** – If your devices show up on Shodan, fix it.
- **Lock down your network** – Segment critical infrastructure.
- **Stop passive & active scanning** – Encrypt, monitor, and detect.
- **Use deception** – Lead attackers into dead ends and honeypots.

At the end of the day, the best cyberattack is the one that never happens. And if an attacker gives up because your smart grid is too hard to hack? Well, then you've already won. Game over. 😺

Chapter 4: Attacking Advanced Metering Infrastructure (AMI)

Smart meters are like nosy neighbors—they constantly monitor electricity usage and report back to the utility company. But what if someone hacked your meter and convinced it that you were only using a fraction of your actual power consumption? Free electricity, anyone? Attackers have discovered all sorts of ways to manipulate AMI networks, from jamming communications to billing fraud schemes that would make any scammer jealous. It's a digital Wild West, and unless we secure these systems, some clever hacker is going to figure out how to turn their entire street into a "free energy zone."

Advanced Metering Infrastructure (AMI) is a critical component of the smart grid, enabling two-way communication between utilities and consumers. However, its reliance on wireless and internet-based communication introduces security risks, such as data manipulation, unauthorized access, and denial-of-service attacks. This chapter examines AMI components, common vulnerabilities, and real-world attack scenarios, while also providing best practices for securing metering networks against exploitation.

4.1 Understanding AMI Components and Data Flow

Alright, let's get one thing straight: Advanced Metering Infrastructure (AMI) is the nervous system of the smart grid. It's how utilities talk to your electricity meter, track your energy usage, and—most importantly—make sure you actually pay for that power-hungry gaming setup.

But here's the kicker: AMI is also a prime target for cyberattacks. Why? Because it's a massive, interconnected network of millions of smart meters, data collectors, and control systems—and hackers love big attack surfaces. If an attacker gains control of AMI, they can do all sorts of fun (and illegal) things, like:

✓☐ Manipulate electricity bills (free power, anyone?)
✓☐ Knock entire neighborhoods offline
✓☐ Intercept and tamper with grid communication
✓☐ Use compromised smart meters as a backdoor into the larger smart grid

So, before we dive into hacking (and defending) AMI, we need to understand how it actually works.

4.1.1 What is AMI?

At its core, AMI is an automated system that enables two-way communication between smart meters and utility companies. Unlike the old-school meters that needed a guy with a clipboard to check them, smart meters talk to the grid in real time.

Key Functions of AMI:

✓☐ **Remote Meter Reading** – No more manual readings. Utilities can pull real-time usage data whenever they want.
✓☐ **Dynamic Pricing** – Electricity rates change based on demand. AMI allows utilities to charge more when the grid is stressed.
✓☐ **Outage Detection** – If power goes out, AMI instantly alerts the utility—no need for you to call in.
✓☐ **Remote Disconnect/Reconnect** – Utilities can cut off or restore power remotely (great for dealing with unpaid bills… or hackers).
✓☐ **Demand Response** – AMI helps balance the grid by adjusting power consumption during peak times.

All of this sounds pretty cool—until you realize that every single one of these features can be exploited if AMI security isn't rock solid.

4.1.2 Components of AMI

1☐ Smart Meters

Think of these as the spies sitting inside every home and business, silently reporting energy usage back to the grid. These devices are packed with microcontrollers, memory, communication modules, and security features—or at least they're supposed to be secure. Many smart meters still use weak encryption, default passwords, or outdated firmware, making them low-hanging fruit for attackers.

2☐ Data Collectors & Aggregators

Not every smart meter talks directly to the utility. Instead, many meters send their data to local data collectors or aggregators, which then pass the information upstream. If an attacker takes over a data collector, they can manipulate data from thousands of meters at once.

3️ Head-End System (HES)

This is the brain of AMI. It's a central system that collects data from all meters, processes it, and forwards it to the utility's billing and control systems. The HES must be highly secure—because if an attacker compromises it, they own the entire AMI network.

4️ Meter Data Management System (MDMS)

This is where all metering data is stored, analyzed, and turned into something useful (like bills). MDMS plays a crucial role in fraud detection, load forecasting, and analytics. But here's the scary part: if an attacker manipulates this data, they can erase usage history, alter bills, or disrupt grid operations.

5️ Communication Networks

AMI relies on various communication technologies, including:

✓️ **Power Line Communication (PLC)** – Uses existing power lines to transmit data.
✓️ **Radio Frequency (RF) Mesh** – Wireless smart meters that relay data to each other.
✓️ **Cellular (3G/4G/5G)** – Some meters use mobile networks to send data.
✓️ **Wi-Fi, Zigbee, LoRa, Wi-SUN** – Used in specific AMI deployments.

Each communication method has its own set of vulnerabilities—and attackers love finding weak spots.

4.1.3 How AMI Data Flows

Understanding AMI data flow is crucial for both securing and attacking the system. Here's how the magic happens:

Step 1: Data Collection

Every smart meter records energy usage in real time and stores it internally.

Step 2: Data Transmission

Meters periodically send encrypted usage data to a data collector or directly to the Head-End System via RF, PLC, or cellular networks.

Step 3: Data Processing

The HES aggregates, normalizes, and processes the data before forwarding it to the Meter Data Management System (MDMS).

Step 4: Billing & Analytics

The MDMS stores the data, runs analytics, and generates electricity bills. This data is also used for grid monitoring, fraud detection, and predictive maintenance.

Step 5: Command & Control

AMI isn't just about sending data to the utility—it also allows utilities to send commands back to smart meters, such as:

✓☐ **Demand response requests** (adjusting power consumption during peak hours)
✓☐ **Remote disconnect/reconnect** (turning power on/off)
✓☐ **Firmware updates & security patches** (assuming they're actually applied…)

If an attacker gains access to this communication loop, they can hijack AMI to manipulate billing, disrupt power, or even shut down the grid.

4.1.4 The Security Risks in AMI Data Flow

Now that we understand how AMI works, let's talk about how it can be attacked. Here are some of the biggest risks:

🔒 Data Interception (MITM Attacks)

If AMI communications aren't encrypted properly, attackers can intercept and modify meter readings, inject false data, or even impersonate the utility.

☐ Unauthorized Access

Weak authentication on smart meters, data collectors, or the HES can allow attackers to:

✓☐ Steal consumer data

✓☐ Change meter configurations
✓☐ Shut down entire AMI networks

💣 Remote Exploits & Malware

Smart meters and AMI servers run firmware and software that can be hacked. Attackers can:

✓☐ Exploit unpatched vulnerabilities
✓☐ Deploy malware to compromise thousands of meters at once
✓☐ Use compromised meters as a botnet for larger grid attacks

🥷 Fraud & Energy Theft

Some attackers hack AMI just to get free electricity. Others sell hacked smart meters that report lower usage—hurting both utilities and legitimate consumers.

Final Thoughts: AMI is Powerful… But Dangerous

AMI is one of the most critical components of the smart grid, providing utilities with unprecedented visibility and control. But with great power comes great hacking potential—and if security isn't airtight, AMI can become a massive liability.

So what's next? Now that we understand AMI's components and data flow, it's time to learn how attackers exploit it—and how to stop them. Buckle up, because the next chapters are about to get even more interesting… and a whole lot scarier. 😺

4.2 Exploiting Smart Meter Vulnerabilities

Alright, let's get one thing straight: smart meters were supposed to make our lives easier—no more meter readers knocking on your door, no more estimated bills, and no more "Oops, we undercharged you for six months, so here's a giant bill." But with great convenience comes great hackability.

Smart meters are tiny computers connected to a massive, complex network. And you know what happens when computers are networked and not properly secured? Hackers have a field day. Whether it's energy theft, billing fraud, or turning off an entire neighborhood's power just for fun, exploiting smart meters is easier than most utilities want to admit.

So, let's dive into how attackers can compromise smart meters, what kind of damage they can cause, and—most importantly—how to stop them.

4.2.1 The Weakest Links in Smart Meters

Smart meters might look like simple devices that measure electricity consumption, but inside, they're packed with firmware, communication modules, and security mechanisms—or at least, they're supposed to be secure. Here are the most common vulnerabilities attackers love to exploit:

1⃞ Default & Hardcoded Credentials

Many smart meters ship with default admin passwords like admin123 or, even worse, 1234. Some manufacturers even hardcode credentials into the firmware, which means an attacker who extracts the firmware can uncover these credentials and use them to take over the meter.

Hacker Tactic:

Use publicly available default passwords to log into meters.

Extract firmware to find hidden backdoor accounts.

2⃞ Weak Encryption or No Encryption at All

Some smart meters don't encrypt their communications properly, meaning attackers can intercept, modify, or replay data packets. This is a goldmine for hackers, allowing them to:
✓⃞ Alter meter readings
✓⃞ Inject fake consumption data
✓⃞ Spoof utility commands

Hacker Tactic:

Perform a Man-in-the-Middle (MITM) attack to modify data in transit.

Capture unencrypted commands and replay them to manipulate the meter.

3️⃣ Firmware Vulnerabilities & Backdoors

Most smart meters run custom firmware developed by vendors. And guess what? That firmware isn't always secure. Unpatched vulnerabilities can allow attackers to:

✓☐ Bypass authentication
✓☐ Upload malicious firmware
✓☐ Gain full control of the meter

Hacker Tactic:

Reverse-engineer the firmware using tools like Binwalk and Ghidra.

Exploit buffer overflows, command injection, or logic flaws.

4️⃣ Physical Access Exploits

If an attacker gets physical access to a smart meter, it's game over. Many meters have debugging ports like UART, JTAG, or SPI that allow direct access to the meter's brain.

Hacker Tactic:

Use a Raspberry Pi or Bus Pirate to connect to debug interfaces.

Dump the firmware and extract sensitive data like encryption keys.

4.2.2 Real-World Smart Meter Hacks

Now, let's look at some real-world attacks on smart meters that show just how vulnerable these devices can be.

🔌 The $24 Million Energy Theft Scam (Spain, 2014)

A hacking group compromised thousands of smart meters across Spain, altering their consumption data to report lower usage. The attackers bypassed security measures and reflashed the firmware to modify meter readings. The total estimated loss? Over $24 million.

🖅 Mass Meter Disconnection Attack (Puerto Rico, 2009)

Hackers successfully tampered with more than 10,000 smart meters, allowing customers to pay less for electricity—or even get it for free. The attackers gained access to the meters' encryption keys and used a laptop to send modified consumption reports back to the grid.

💡 Smart Meter Worm Attack (Theoretical, But Scary!)

Researchers have demonstrated that self-propagating malware can spread between smart meters, just like a computer worm. A single infected meter could spread malicious code throughout an entire AMI network, leading to mass meter failures or coordinated power disruptions.

4.2.3 How Attackers Exploit Smart Meters

Now, let's break down the step-by-step process hackers use to exploit smart meters.

Step 1: Reconnaissance & Target Selection

Hackers first identify which meters are vulnerable by:

✓☐ Scanning public databases (like Shodan or Censys) for exposed AMI networks.
✓☐ Using RF sniffers to capture wireless smart meter communications.
✓☐ Physically inspecting meters to find debug ports or weak points.

Step 2: Reverse Engineering the Firmware

If the attacker gets hold of a meter or its firmware, they will:

✓☐ Dump the firmware using JTAG, SPI, or UART.
✓☐ Analyze the firmware with Binwalk, Ghidra, or IDA Pro.
✓☐ Look for backdoor accounts, weak encryption, or authentication flaws.

Step 3: Exploiting the Meter

Once vulnerabilities are identified, the attacker can:

✓☐ Modify energy consumption to pay lower bills.
✓☐ Shut off power remotely by exploiting remote disconnect features.
✓☐ Use compromised meters as a pivot point to attack the larger grid.

Step 4: Covering Their Tracks

A smart attacker will:

✓☐ Erase logs or overwrite firmware to hide their actions.
✓☐ Use encrypted tunnels to avoid detection.
✓☐ Deploy backdoors so they can return whenever they want.

4.2.4 Defending Against Smart Meter Attacks

So, how do we secure smart meters from these kinds of attacks?

1☐ Secure Authentication & Encryption

✓☐ Implement strong, unique passwords and disable default credentials.
✓☐ Use end-to-end encryption for meter communications.
✓☐ Enforce multi-factor authentication (MFA) for remote access.

2☐ Regular Firmware Updates & Security Patches

✓☐ Apply security patches ASAP—don't wait for an attack to happen.
✓☐ Implement secure boot to prevent unauthorized firmware modifications.

3☐ Physical Security Hardening

✓☐ Protect debug ports (UART, JTAG) with tamper-evident seals.
✓☐ Use anti-tampering circuits to detect unauthorized modifications.

4☐ Anomaly Detection & Intrusion Prevention

✓☐ Deploy AI-driven anomaly detection to spot unusual consumption patterns.
✓☐ Monitor AMI traffic for unauthorized access attempts.

✓☐ Use honeypots to detect active smart meter attacks.

Final Thoughts: Smart Meters = Smart Targets

Smart meters are here to stay, but they must be secured—because hackers aren't just interested in stealing power; they're looking for ways to take down the entire grid.

If we don't prioritize security, we'll see more large-scale attacks, more energy fraud, and more blackouts. So, whether you're a security professional, a utility company, or just someone who doesn't want their power shut off by a teenager with a laptop—we all have a stake in securing AMI.

Next up? More attacks, more exploits, and (hopefully) more ways to stop them. Let's keep the lights on. 💡😺

4.3 Manipulating Energy Consumption Data and Billing Fraud

Alright, let's be honest—who hasn't dreamed of cutting their electricity bill in half? Maybe even getting free electricity? Well, cybercriminals have that dream too, and unfortunately, they know exactly how to make it a reality.

Tampering with energy consumption data isn't just a hacker's fantasy—it's a real-world cybercrime that costs utility companies billions of dollars every year. From modifying smart meter readings to spoofing entire billing systems, attackers have found ways to game the system while staying under the radar. And trust me, it's not just a bunch of script kiddies trying to get free Netflix power—organized crime syndicates and even nation-state actors have been caught in large-scale electricity fraud schemes.

So, let's dive into how energy billing fraud works, the techniques attackers use, and (most importantly) how to stop them.

4.3.1 The Many Flavors of Energy Fraud

There are several ways to manipulate energy consumption data, and each comes with its own level of risk and sophistication. Here are the most common methods:

1☐ Firmware Manipulation

Smart meters run firmware, just like any other IoT device. If an attacker can reverse-engineer the firmware and modify its logic, they can:

✓☐ Alter energy consumption reports to show lower usage.
✓☐ Disable remote disconnection features so utilities can't cut power.
✓☐ Bypass tamper detection so no one knows it was hacked.

Hacker Tactic:

Dump the firmware using JTAG, UART, or SPI ports.

Reverse-engineer it with tools like Binwalk, Ghidra, or IDA Pro.

Patch the firmware to report fake consumption values.

Reflash the modified firmware back onto the meter.

🚨 **Real-World Example:**

In Spain, hackers compromised thousands of smart meters by modifying firmware. The utility lost $24 million before realizing something was off.

2☐ Man-in-the-Middle (MITM) Attacks on Meter Data

Smart meters communicate with utilities using protocols like DLMS/COSEM, Modbus, and MQTT. If encryption and authentication are weak (or nonexistent), attackers can:

✓☐ Intercept and modify meter readings before they reach the utility.
✓☐ Spoof utility commands to reset usage data.
✓☐ Replay old consumption values to hide tampering.

Hacker Tactic:

Use a Raspberry Pi or HackRF to sniff wireless smart meter traffic.

Inject modified data before it reaches the utility's billing system.

Trick the system into believing the customer barely used any power.

🚨 Real-World Example:

Hackers in Puerto Rico successfully intercepted and altered smart meter data, allowing customers to reduce their energy bills by up to 75%.

3️⃣ Remote Access Exploits & Credential Theft

Some utility companies have terrible security hygiene—think default passwords, hardcoded credentials, and unpatched remote access servers. If attackers gain access to the utility's AMI or SCADA systems, they can:

✓ Mass-edit billing data to reduce or erase consumption records.
✓ Create fake accounts that get power without ever paying.
✓ Take over the utility's billing system and sell discounted electricity to customers.

Hacker Tactic:

Use Shodan or Censys to find exposed AMI endpoints.

Bruteforce login credentials or exploit unpatched web applications.

Modify or delete customer billing records inside the database.

🚨 Real-World Example:

A cybercriminal group hacked into a South American utility's billing system, altered customer records, and offered to cut electricity bills for a fee.

4️⃣ Physical Smart Meter Tampering

Sometimes, hackers don't need sophisticated cyberattacks—a screwdriver and some electronics skills can get the job done. By physically tampering with smart meters, attackers can:

✓ Slow down the meter's internal clock to report less consumption.
✓ Insert magnets or resistors to interfere with current measurements.
✓ Bypass the meter entirely by rewiring circuits inside a home or business.

Hacker Tactic:

Open the meter casing and disable tamper sensors.

Attach a small neodymium magnet to disrupt current flow measurements.

Modify voltage regulators to reduce recorded energy usage.

🔍 Real-World Example:

In India, electricity theft through physical meter tampering is estimated to cost utilities over $16 billion per year.

4.3.2 Why Energy Fraud is a Big Deal

You might be thinking:

"So what? Some guy in a basement shaves a few bucks off his electric bill—who cares?"

Well, utilities do. A LOT.

Financial Impact

Billing fraud costs utility companies billions of dollars annually. And guess what? That loss isn't just absorbed—it gets passed down to paying customers in the form of higher energy prices.

Grid Stability Issues

When large-scale fraud occurs, utilities lose visibility into how much electricity is actually being consumed. This leads to:

⚡ Overloaded substations
⚡ Voltage fluctuations
⚡ Unstable grid conditions that can cause blackouts

Cybercrime Syndicates & Terrorism

Energy fraud isn't just a small-time scam—organized crime groups and even nation-state actors have been involved in smart meter hacking. Some groups offer fraud-as-a-service, selling hacked smart meters to customers who want to avoid paying their bills.

4.3.3 Stopping Smart Meter Fraud: Defensive Strategies

Now for the good part—how do we stop this madness?

1️ Secure Firmware & Tamper Detection

✓ Implement secure boot to prevent unauthorized firmware modifications.
✓ Use tamper-evident seals and sensors to detect physical attacks.
✓ Encrypt firmware updates to prevent malicious flashing.

2️ Strong Encryption & Authentication

✓ Enforce end-to-end encryption (TLS, AES-256) for meter communications.
✓ Use certificate-based authentication to verify legitimate meters.
✓ Regularly rotate encryption keys to prevent replay attacks.

3️ AI-Powered Anomaly Detection

✓ Deploy machine learning models to detect abnormal consumption patterns.
✓ Use honeypots—fake smart meters designed to attract hackers and track their methods.
✓ Monitor for sudden usage drops, which may indicate fraud.

4️ Better Physical Security

✓ Install hardened smart meters with protected debug interfaces.
✓ Use RF shielding to prevent wireless MITM attacks.
✓ Implement geofencing to detect if a meter has been moved or tampered with.

Final Thoughts: The Battle Between Hackers & Utilities

Look, hackers and utilities are locked in a never-ending game of cat and mouse. Every time a new security measure is deployed, attackers find a creative way around it. Billing fraud will never fully disappear, but strong cybersecurity practices can make it a hell of a lot harder.

So, if you're a security professional, a utility worker, or just someone who actually pays their electricity bill—staying ahead of these attacks is crucial.

Up next? Even more smart grid attacks, exploits, and defenses. Stay charged. 🔋😼

4.4 Jamming and Spoofing AMI Communications

Ever wished you could just mute your electricity bill like an annoying group chat? Well, cybercriminals are way ahead of you! By jamming and spoofing Advanced Metering Infrastructure (AMI) communications, they can mess with the smart grid, disrupt energy readings, and even cause billing chaos.

Imagine this: a hacker parks outside your house, sends a few rogue radio signals, and suddenly—boom! Your smart meter stops sending data. No bill. No record of usage. Free electricity! Sounds fun, right? Well, utilities don't think so. This kind of attack doesn't just let some guy run his PlayStation for free—it can cripple entire grid operations if done at scale.

In this section, we'll dive into how hackers jam and spoof AMI communications, real-world attacks, and how to stop them before the lights go out (for real).

4.4.1 How AMI Communications Work (And Why They're Vulnerable)

AMI systems rely on wireless communication to send meter data back to utility companies. This usually involves RF mesh networks, cellular IoT (NB-IoT, LTE-M), Zigbee, LoRa, and PLC (Power Line Communication).

Here's the problem: radio signals are easy to jam, intercept, and manipulate. If a hacker can disrupt AMI communications, they can:

✓☐ Prevent meters from sending usage data (billing disruption).
✓☐ Send fake meter readings (energy fraud).
✓☐ Cause mass confusion for utilities (potential blackout conditions).

Now, let's talk about the two most common attacks: jamming and spoofing.

4.4.2 Jamming AMI Signals: The Cybercriminal's Mute Button

What is Jamming?

Jamming is like blasting death metal at full volume during a conference call—no one can hear anything. By overwhelming the wireless frequency used by smart meters with high-power noise, attackers can completely block communication between meters and the grid.

How Hackers Jam Smart Meters

Identify the target frequency (using SDR tools like HackRF, RTL-SDR, or BladeRF).

Generate high-power interference (using a simple RF transmitter).

Block AMI network communication, making meters unable to report usage.

Real-World Example

A hacker in Texas used a $30 RF jammer to knock out an entire neighborhood's AMI meters. The result? No one got billed for months! The utility had to physically visit each house to reset the meters.

4.4.3 Spoofing AMI Communications: Sending Fake Data

What is Spoofing?

Spoofing is like photoshopping your driver's license to say you're 21 when you're really 16. Attackers send fake meter readings to the utility to manipulate billing or hide energy theft.

How Hackers Spoof AMI Meters

Intercept smart meter packets using SDR tools.

Modify the data (reduce consumption, inject fake timestamps, etc.).

Replay the altered packets to the utility network.

Real-World Example

In Puerto Rico, hackers used AMI spoofing to lower thousands of electricity bills. Some people were paying $5 per month for industrial-scale power consumption. The fraud cost utilities hundreds of millions before they figured it out.

4.4.4 Consequences of Jamming & Spoofing Attacks

These attacks might sound like a hacker's dream, but they have serious consequences:

⚠️ **Billing Chaos**: Utilities can't charge customers correctly if meter data is blocked or spoofed.

⚠️ **Grid Instability**: Unreported energy consumption can lead to miscalculations in power distribution, risking outages.

⚠️ **Regulatory Violations**: Many regions have strict laws around smart grid security, and utilities can face massive fines if they don't protect AMI communications.

⚠️ **Criminal Exploitation**: Organized crime groups can sell energy fraud as a service, offering people "discounted" electricity through illegal hacking.

4.4.5 How to Defend Against Jamming & Spoofing

Now that we know how bad things can get, let's talk defense.

1️⃣ Anti-Jamming Measures

✓ **Frequency Hopping Spread Spectrum (FHSS):** This makes the meter constantly switch frequencies, making it harder to jam.

✓ **Adaptive Power Control**: Reducing transmission power in noisy environments helps minimize interference.

✓ **Jamming Detection Systems**: Utilities should monitor for unusual RF interference patterns.

2️⃣ Anti-Spoofing Measures

✓ **Strong Encryption (AES-256, TLS 1.3):** Prevents attackers from modifying meter data.

✓ **Message Authentication Codes (MACs):** Ensures that only legitimate meters can send data.

✓☐ **Anomaly Detection Algorithms**: AI-powered tools can spot unusual energy usage trends and flag potential spoofing.

3☐ Physical Security Upgrades

✓☐ **Shielding**: Adding RF shielding to AMI meters can reduce interference.
✓☐ **Tamper Detection**: Smart meters should log any unauthorized access attempts.
✓☐ **Remote Meter Resets**: Utilities should be able to reset or reauthenticate meters remotely after suspected attacks.

Final Thoughts: The Never-Ending Cat & Mouse Game

Cybercriminals are constantly evolving their attacks, and AMI networks are a prime target because of their wireless nature. Jamming and spoofing aren't just theoretical—they're happening in the real world.

If you're a utility provider, a security researcher, or just someone who enjoys not living in a blackout, it's time to take these threats seriously.

Next up? Even more smart grid hacking tactics—and how to stop them. Stay tuned! 😼 🔌

4.5 Securing AMI Networks from Cyber Threats

Alright, folks—by now, we've seen just how wild the world of Advanced Metering Infrastructure (AMI) security can get. Hackers jamming signals like they're at a rock concert, spoofing meter readings to cut their bills down to a couple of bucks, and turning entire neighborhoods into "free electricity zones" (until the utility company catches on). It's like a cyberpunk thriller, except the villain is some guy in his garage with a software-defined radio and way too much free time.

But fear not! We're not about to let the bad guys win. This chapter is all about how to secure AMI networks—locking down communication channels, fortifying meters, and making sure energy thieves have to go back to good old-fashioned extension cord trickery.

4.5.1 Why Securing AMI is So Hard (But Necessary)

AMI networks are tricky to secure because they rely on wireless communication, which makes them naturally susceptible to eavesdropping, jamming, and spoofing attacks. Plus, many meters and AMI devices are built for efficiency and cost-effectiveness—which means security often takes a backseat.

The risks?

⚠️ **Billing Fraud**: Attackers manipulate meter readings to lower their energy bills or create fake usage records.

⚠️ **Grid Instability**: A compromised AMI system can disrupt power distribution, leading to outages and blackouts.

⚠️ **Unauthorized Access**: Hackers can use AMI vulnerabilities to gain a foothold into SCADA and critical infrastructure systems.

⚠️ **Privacy Violations**: AMI collects detailed consumer energy usage data, which can be exploited to profile users or even predict when they're home.

Clearly, security is not optional—it's critical.

4.5.2 Securing AMI Communications

🔒 **Encrypt Everything (No, Seriously. EVERYTHING.)**

Encryption is the first and most crucial defense. If attackers manage to intercept AMI data, we want them to get a garbled mess of nonsense instead of anything useful.

Use AES-256 encryption for smart meter data transmission.

TLS 1.3 for network connections to secure communication between meters and head-end systems.

End-to-End Encryption (E2EE) ensures that even if data is intercepted mid-transmission, it remains protected.

Without encryption, AMI security is basically like leaving your Wi-Fi password written on your front door.

🔑 **Use Secure Authentication (Because Password123 is Not Enough)**

Every smart meter and AMI device should authenticate itself before transmitting data. Otherwise, an attacker could simply pretend to be a legitimate meter and start sending fake readings.

Public Key Infrastructure (PKI): Each device gets a unique cryptographic key.

Mutual Authentication: The meter verifies the utility company, and the utility verifies the meter—no imposters allowed!

Certificate-Based Security: Devices should use X.509 certificates to prove their identity.

Imagine walking into a secure facility and saying, "Trust me, I work here." That's what weak authentication looks like in AMI networks.

🛡 Defending Against Jamming & Spoofing Attacks

We covered how attackers jam and spoof AMI signals in the last section. Now, let's talk about how to fight back.

✅ **Frequency Hopping Spread Spectrum (FHSS):** Instead of staying on a single frequency (where it can be jammed easily), FHSS rapidly switches channels, making interference much harder.
✅ **Adaptive Power Control**: If interference is detected, smart meters should adjust transmission power dynamically to avoid complete signal loss.
✅ **Anomaly Detection Algorithms**: If a meter suddenly goes silent or starts sending strange data, the system should flag it for investigation.

Think of it like a boxer dodging punches—by constantly moving and adapting, it's much harder to get knocked out.

4.5.3 Hardening Smart Meters and AMI Devices

🔒 Physical Security Matters

You'd be amazed how many "cyber" attacks start with just opening up a device. Smart meters should have:

♦ Tamper detection mechanisms (alerts if someone tries to open the casing).
♦ Secure boot technology (so only authorized firmware can run on the device).

◆ Hardware security modules (HSMs) to store cryptographic keys securely.

Why does this matter? Because if an attacker can physically extract encryption keys from one meter, they can potentially compromise the entire AMI network.

☐ **Secure Firmware Updates (No More Zombie Meters)**

A smart meter with outdated firmware is a hacker's playground.

To prevent this:

✓☐ Use digitally signed firmware updates (to prevent unauthorized code from being installed).

✓☐ Enable remote updates, but only if they're encrypted and authenticated.

✓☐ Implement rollback protection so attackers can't force old, vulnerable firmware versions to be reinstalled.

If firmware isn't updated regularly, smart meters become security fossils—outdated, fragile, and easy to exploit.

4.5.4 Network Monitoring and Intrusion Detection

Even with all the protections in place, you need to watch for suspicious activity in AMI networks.

Network Intrusion Detection Systems (NIDS): These monitor AMI traffic for unusual patterns (e.g., meters suddenly going offline, data being replayed, etc.).

AI and Machine Learning-Based Threat Detection: AI can identify billing anomalies, unusual consumption trends, and jamming signals faster than humans.

Automated Incident Response: If an attack is detected, systems should automatically block suspicious devices or re-authenticate them before restoring service.

Because no security system is perfect, constant monitoring and fast response are essential.

4.5.5 Regulatory Compliance: Making Sure AMI Security is More Than an Afterthought

Security isn't just about keeping hackers out—it's also about staying compliant with industry regulations.

📕 **NERC CIP**: Requires utilities to secure bulk electric systems from cyber threats.
📕 **IEC 62443**: Establishes best practices for industrial control system security.
📕 **ISO 27019**: Provides guidelines for managing smart grid cybersecurity.

By following these standards, utilities not only reduce cyber risks but also avoid massive fines and legal trouble.

Final Thoughts: Keeping the Lights On (Literally)

Securing AMI networks is like fortifying a castle—you need strong walls (encryption), guarded gates (authentication), hidden escape routes (backup measures), and vigilant watchtowers (monitoring).

Hackers will keep trying to exploit AMI weaknesses, but by locking down communications, hardening devices, and staying ahead of emerging threats, we can make their job a lot harder.

So, to all the security pros, penetration testers, and engineers out there—let's keep the grid safe, one meter at a time. Because nobody wants to wake up one morning and find out their city's power got hacked by a kid with a laptop and a radio transmitter. 😊 🔌

Chapter 5: Exploiting SCADA and Industrial Control Systems (ICS)

If smart meters are the foot soldiers of the grid, SCADA systems are the generals calling the shots. Unfortunately, many of these "generals" are running on outdated protocols, weak authentication, and sometimes even default passwords (seriously?). Hackers have already proven they can infiltrate ICS environments, manipulate circuit breakers, and even cause large-scale blackouts. Remember Stuxnet? That wasn't a fluke—that was a playbook. And trust me, others have been taking notes.

Supervisory Control and Data Acquisition (SCADA) and Industrial Control Systems (ICS) are the backbone of power grid operations, responsible for managing power generation, transmission, and distribution. However, these systems were not originally designed with cybersecurity in mind, making them susceptible to MITM attacks, unauthorized access, and malware infections. This chapter delves into ICS attack vectors, real-world breaches, and the defensive measures necessary to protect critical infrastructure.

5.1 Understanding SCADA, ICS, and Their Role in the Smart Grid

Alright, let's start with a quick reality check—when most people hear "hacking the power grid," they imagine some hoodie-wearing genius hammering away on a keyboard while green numbers scroll down their screen like a scene from The Matrix.

In reality? It's often way simpler than that. A misconfigured SCADA system, an exposed ICS device, or an outdated industrial protocol running without encryption—these are the real backdoors into critical infrastructure. And that's what we're here to talk about.

Supervisory Control and Data Acquisition (SCADA) and Industrial Control Systems (ICS) are the brains and nervous system of the smart grid. They make sure electricity gets generated, transmitted, and distributed without total chaos. But the problem? These systems were built before cybersecurity was even a thing.

Let's break it down and see how SCADA, ICS, and the smart grid all fit together—before we dive into the many ways hackers love to mess with them.

5.1.1 What is SCADA?

Imagine you're running a massive power grid. You've got:

Power plants generating electricity

Transmission lines moving power long distances

Distribution systems delivering it to homes and businesses

Now, how do you monitor and control all of this without having people physically stationed at every single power plant, substation, and transformer?

That's where SCADA (Supervisory Control and Data Acquisition) comes in.

SCADA is a system of software and hardware that allows operators to remotely monitor and control industrial processes. It collects real-time data, sends commands, and automates critical operations.

SCADA Components

SCADA isn't just one thing—it's a network of interconnected parts:

Remote Terminal Units (RTUs): These little guys collect data from sensors and send it back to a control center.

Programmable Logic Controllers (PLCs): Think of these as small industrial computers that execute commands (e.g., open a circuit breaker, adjust a generator).

Human-Machine Interfaces (HMIs): The screens operators use to see what's happening and control the grid.

SCADA Servers & Control Centers: These systems process data from RTUs and PLCs and allow human operators to make decisions.

Why SCADA is Critical for the Smart Grid

Without SCADA, power grids would be like a massive orchestra with no conductor. SCADA helps:

✅ Monitor voltage, frequency, and grid stability in real time.

✅ Detect and respond to faults automatically (so your lights don't flicker every time a squirrel meets an unfortunate end on a transformer).

✅ Remotely manage substations and grid assets, reducing the need for field workers.

Great, so SCADA is basically the central nervous system of the power grid. Now let's talk about the organs and muscles—the Industrial Control Systems (ICS).

5.1.2 What are Industrial Control Systems (ICS)?

Industrial Control Systems (ICS) is a broad term that includes SCADA, Distributed Control Systems (DCS), and other automation technologies used in industrial environments.

If SCADA is the "overseer," then ICS components are the actual doers—they execute commands and keep everything running smoothly.

Types of ICS

💡 **SCADA Systems** – Used in large-scale operations like power grids, water treatment plants, and pipelines.

💡 **DCS (Distributed Control Systems)** – Found in industries like oil refineries and manufacturing plants where processes are highly localized.

💡 **PLC-Based Control Systems** – Used in factories, substations, and small-scale industrial setups.

For smart grids, ICS is critical for real-time automation. It allows systems to:

✅ Adjust power generation dynamically based on demand.

✅ Detect and fix faults faster than human operators ever could.

✅ Integrate renewable energy sources (solar, wind) into the grid seamlessly.

But here's the catch: Most ICS devices were never designed with cybersecurity in mind.

5.1.3 How SCADA and ICS Fit Into the Smart Grid

Now that we know what SCADA and ICS are, let's see how they fit into the bigger picture of the modern smart grid.

The Three Layers of a Smart Grid

1☐ **Generation Layer** – Power plants, renewable energy farms, and other energy sources create electricity. SCADA is used here to monitor generation efficiency, manage loads, and optimize output.

2☐ **Transmission Layer** – High-voltage transmission lines move electricity across vast distances. SCADA systems control switchgear, relays, and circuit breakers to ensure power flows without blackouts.

3☐ **Distribution Layer** – Substations and local networks deliver electricity to homes and businesses. ICS controls smart meters, automated transformers, and energy storage systems.

The problem? Each of these layers is an attack surface for cyber threats.

If a hacker takes control of a SCADA system in the Generation Layer, they could cause massive blackouts.

If they manipulate the Transmission Layer, they could overload lines, damage equipment, and trigger cascading failures.

In the Distribution Layer, attackers can alter smart meters, disrupt billing systems, or cause localized outages.

Simply put: SCADA and ICS are the backbone of the smart grid, and if they're compromised, the entire power system is at risk.

5.1.4 The Big Problem: SCADA and ICS Were Never Built for Cybersecurity

Here's the scary truth—most SCADA and ICS systems were designed decades ago, when cybersecurity wasn't even a thought. These systems were built for availability and reliability, not security.

And that means:

🔒 Many SCADA protocols don't use encryption or authentication—making them easy to intercept and manipulate.

🏧 Remote access is often enabled by default, allowing attackers to control grid operations from anywhere.

🏧 Legacy devices lack firmware updates, leaving them vulnerable to exploits that have been known for years.

The result? SCADA and ICS systems have become prime targets for hackers, nation-state attackers, and cybercriminals.

5.1.5 The Road Ahead: Securing SCADA and ICS in the Smart Grid

So what's the solution? Hardening SCADA and ICS systems is essential to prevent cyber threats from disrupting the smart grid.

Here's how:

🔐 **Implement Strong Authentication** – Require multi-factor authentication (MFA) for remote access to SCADA systems.

🛡 **Use Network Segmentation** – Keep SCADA networks separate from corporate IT networks to prevent lateral movement.

🔒 **Encrypt SCADA Communications** – Deploy TLS and VPNs to secure data transmission.

📊 **Monitor for Anomalies** – Use Intrusion Detection Systems (IDS) to detect unusual activity in SCADA networks.

🔄 **Regularly Update Firmware & Patch Vulnerabilities** – Yes, even industrial systems need updates!

SCADA and ICS security isn't just an IT problem—it's a national security issue. If attackers can control the grid, they control everything.

Final Thoughts: The Smart Grid's Greatest Weakness? Outdated Thinking.

SCADA and ICS are absolutely essential to keeping our lights on, our industries running, and our cities powered. But as the smart grid evolves, so do the threats against it.

It's time to move beyond outdated security assumptions and start treating SCADA and ICS like what they are—critical infrastructure that needs to be defended at all costs. Because the alternative? A hacker in another country pressing a button and turning your entire city into a blackout zone. 🏧 💡

5.2 Attacking Legacy ICS Protocols and Unpatched Systems

Let's be honest—legacy Industrial Control System (ICS) protocols are like your grandpa's old flip phone. It still works, but put it up against modern security threats, and it's about as useful as a chocolate teapot.

For decades, ICS protocols were designed for reliability and efficiency, not cybersecurity. They were built assuming that only trusted people and devices would ever communicate with them. Fast forward to today, and these same systems are connected to the internet, remotely accessible, and riddled with vulnerabilities. Hackers love this. It's like they've been handed the keys to the power grid, and the locks are all rusty.

In this chapter, we'll explore why legacy ICS protocols are dangerously outdated, how attackers exploit them, and what can be done to defend against these threats. Let's dive in.

5.2.1 The Problem with Legacy ICS Protocols

1. No Authentication or Weak Authentication

Many legacy ICS protocols, such as Modbus, DNP3, and OPC Classic, were built at a time when the idea of a hacker sitting in their basement attacking a power grid was pure science fiction.

Modbus: Sends commands with zero authentication—meaning anyone who can talk to the device can control it.

DNP3 (without Secure Authentication): Lacks strong identity verification, making it susceptible to Man-in-the-Middle (MITM) attacks.

OPC Classic: Uses outdated Windows authentication methods, which attackers can easily bypass.

It's like leaving your house unlocked and assuming no one will ever check the doorknob. Spoiler alert: they will.

2. No Encryption = Eavesdropping Made Easy

These legacy protocols send everything in plain text. That means if an attacker gets access to the network (via Wi-Fi sniffing, a compromised router, or a misconfigured firewall), they can read every single command being sent between ICS devices.

Imagine your bank sending your credit card details over email with no encryption. You'd panic, right? Well, critical infrastructure systems are doing this every day.

3. Designed for Closed Networks (Which No Longer Exist)

ICS protocols were built for isolated, air-gapped networks—meaning they were never meant to be connected to the internet or corporate IT networks.

But today, companies want remote access, cloud-based monitoring, and smart automation. This means ICS networks are now exposed to external threats, and these old protocols were never designed to defend against them.

5.2.2 How Hackers Exploit Unpatched ICS Systems

Okay, so we've established that these legacy protocols are full of holes. Now, let's look at how attackers take advantage of them.

1. Man-in-the-Middle (MITM) Attacks

Because legacy ICS protocols lack encryption, attackers can intercept and modify traffic using tools like Ettercap, Wireshark, and MITMf.

💀 Real-world example:

An attacker positions themselves between a control center and a substation, altering SCADA commands to open a circuit breaker, causing a power outage.

2. Replay Attacks

If ICS devices don't verify message authenticity, an attacker can record a legitimate command (like "open breaker") and play it back later.

💀 Real-world example:

A hacker captures "increase turbine speed" commands at a power plant and replays them at a dangerous level—causing mechanical failure.

3. Default or Hardcoded Credentials

Many ICS devices still ship with default admin usernames and passwords, which are often publicly documented.

💀 Real-world example:

Attackers use Shodan to find internet-exposed ICS devices and log in with factory-default credentials. Now they have full control over a water treatment facility or a power grid.

4. Buffer Overflow and Memory Corruption Exploits

Unpatched ICS devices often have known software vulnerabilities, which can be exploited to crash systems or gain unauthorized access.

💀 Real-world example:

A vulnerability in a PLC's firmware allows attackers to send a malformed packet, crashing the device and causing a factory shutdown.

5.2.3 Notable ICS Attacks in History

⚡ Stuxnet (2010) – The Most Infamous ICS Attack

Stuxnet targeted Siemens PLCs in Iran's nuclear facilities, exploiting zero-day vulnerabilities to silently alter centrifuge speeds while displaying normal readings to operators. The result? Centrifuges spun themselves into destruction.

⚡ Industroyer (2016) – Taking Down a Power Grid

Industroyer was designed to attack ICS protocols like IEC 60870-5-104 and OPC-UA. It disrupted Ukraine's power grid, leaving thousands in darkness.

⚡ Triton (2017) – Safety System Sabotage

Triton targeted Schneider Electric's Triconex safety systems in an attempt to disable critical safety functions at an oil refinery—putting lives at risk.

5.2.4 How to Defend Against Legacy ICS Attacks

So, how do we stop attackers from turning our critical infrastructure into a hacker's playground?

1. Patch and Update (If Possible)
Many ICS devices remain unpatched for years due to fears of downtime. But running unpatched systems is like refusing a vaccine in the middle of a pandemic.

Whenever possible, update firmware and software to the latest versions.

2. Implement Network Segmentation

Keep SCADA and ICS networks separate from corporate IT networks.

Use firewalls and VLANs to restrict communication between different network layers.

3. Deploy Secure ICS Protocols (or Wrap Them in Encryption)

Use DNP3 Secure Authentication instead of regular DNP3.

If legacy protocols must be used, wrap them in VPNs or TLS encryption tunnels to prevent eavesdropping.

4. Implement Multi-Factor Authentication (MFA) and Strong Passwords

Eliminate default passwords on ICS devices.

Use MFA for remote access (yes, even for SCADA engineers).

5. Monitor for Anomalous Behavior

Deploy Intrusion Detection Systems (IDS) for ICS traffic, like Snort, Suricata, or Zeek.

Use machine learning-based anomaly detection to spot unexpected behavior in ICS networks.

6. Regularly Test Your ICS Security

Conduct penetration testing and vulnerability assessments to find weaknesses before attackers do.

Run red team exercises simulating real-world ICS attacks.

Final Thoughts: Old Tech, New Risks

ICS protocols were built in a simpler time, but the world has changed. Attackers are smarter, bolder, and better equipped than ever before.

If we don't patch, encrypt, and secure these systems, it's only a matter of time before we see another Stuxnet, another Industroyer, another cyber-physical catastrophe.

So the question isn't if these vulnerabilities will be exploited. The question is who gets there first—us or the attackers? 💀

5.3 MITM Attacks on SCADA Systems and Remote Terminals

Alright, imagine this: you're sitting in a SCADA control room, sipping coffee, monitoring a power grid, thinking everything is fine. Meanwhile, a hacker halfway across the world— or worse, some guy parked outside the facility in a van—is silently intercepting and modifying every command you send. Welcome to the world of Man-in-the-Middle (MITM) attacks on SCADA systems.

MITM attacks are like a sneaky waiter at a restaurant, listening in on your order, changing it before it reaches the kitchen, and then serving you something completely different. Except in this case, instead of an extra-spicy taco, you might get a substation shutting down or a water treatment plant flooding a city. Not so funny now, huh?

In this chapter, we'll break down how MITM attacks work, why SCADA and remote terminal units (RTUs) are vulnerable, real-world attack scenarios, and how to defend against them. Let's dive in.

5.3.1 What is a MITM Attack?

A Man-in-the-Middle (MITM) attack happens when an attacker secretly intercepts, modifies, or relays communication between two parties without their knowledge. The goal? Eavesdrop, manipulate, or completely hijack the communication.

For example, in a SCADA system, an MITM attacker can:

Modify control commands (e.g., change "open valve" to "close valve").

Fake sensor data (e.g., make a turbine look like it's running fine when it's actually overheating).

Steal credentials by capturing login attempts.

Launch replay attacks, where they capture a legitimate command and replay it later.

5.3.2 Why Are SCADA Systems Vulnerable to MITM Attacks?

SCADA networks were designed for reliability, not security. Many of them still use legacy protocols that lack encryption and authentication, making MITM attacks ridiculously easy.

1. No Encryption = Attackers Can Read Everything

Many SCADA protocols, such as Modbus, DNP3, and IEC 60870-5-104, send data in plain text. This means an attacker sniffing the network can see every command and response.

Think about it—would you send your banking password in a postcard? No! But critical infrastructure still does exactly this, sending life-or-death commands in an unprotected format.

2. Weak or Non-Existent Authentication

Some SCADA systems don't verify who is sending commands. This means if an attacker injects fake control signals, the system just accepts them—no questions asked.

3. Outdated and Insecure Remote Access

Many SCADA systems allow remote access through poorly secured VPNs, default credentials, or exposed remote desktop connections. Once attackers gain access, they can perform MITM attacks from anywhere in the world.

4. Insecure Network Architectures

SCADA systems were never designed to be connected to IT networks or the internet, but modern organizations want remote monitoring, cloud access, and real-time analytics. The problem? More connectivity = more attack surfaces.

5.3.3 How Attackers Perform MITM on SCADA Networks

Attackers use different techniques to insert themselves between SCADA components. Here are some of the most common methods:

1. ARP Spoofing (Local Network Hijack)

If an attacker gains access to a SCADA network, they can use ARP spoofing to trick devices into sending traffic through their machine.

💀 Example Attack Scenario:

The SCADA server wants to talk to an RTU.

The attacker tells both devices: "Hey, I'm your gateway!"

The SCADA server unknowingly sends data through the attacker, who modifies or blocks critical commands.

2. DNS Spoofing (Redirecting SCADA Traffic)

If a SCADA system relies on domain names (e.g., scada.company.com), attackers can poison DNS responses, redirecting traffic to a malicious server.

💀 Example Attack Scenario:

The SCADA operator tries to connect to scada.company.com.

The attacker tricks the DNS server into responding with a fake IP address.

The operator unknowingly logs into a fake SCADA system controlled by the attacker.

3. Rogue Wireless Access Points

If SCADA devices use Wi-Fi or cellular connections, an attacker can set up a fake access point (Evil Twin Attack) to intercept traffic.

☠ Example Attack Scenario:

An attacker sets up a fake Wi-Fi access point with the same name as the SCADA network.

RTUs or operator workstations unknowingly connect to it.

The attacker captures and modifies SCADA traffic in real-time.

4. BGP Hijacking (Internet-Level MITM Attack)

Some SCADA traffic flows over the internet, especially for remote substations. Attackers can hijack BGP routes, rerouting SCADA traffic through their own servers.

☠ Example Attack Scenario:

An attacker manipulates internet routing tables to divert SCADA data through a compromised server.

They inject false readings or control commands into the SCADA system.

5.3.4 Real-World MITM Attacks on SCADA Systems

Case Study: Ukraine Power Grid Attack (2015 & 2016)

In two separate attacks, Russian hackers used MITM techniques to hijack SCADA controls, shutting down Ukraine's power grid. They:

Intercepted SCADA traffic to learn how the system worked.

Injected malicious commands to turn off substations.

Locked out operators by changing passwords.

The result?

Hundreds of thousands of people were left in the dark.

5.3.5 How to Defend Against MITM Attacks on SCADA

Stopping MITM attacks isn't easy, but there are several key defenses organizations can implement:

1. Encrypt SCADA Traffic (Even if the Protocol Doesn't Support It)

Use TLS or VPN tunnels to wrap unencrypted SCADA traffic in a secure layer.

Upgrade to secure versions of protocols, such as DNP3 Secure Authentication.

2. Implement Strong Authentication

Enforce multi-factor authentication (MFA) for SCADA operators.

Use mutual authentication between SCADA systems and RTUs to prevent imposters.

3. Network Segmentation

Keep SCADA networks isolated from IT and the internet.

Use firewalls and VLANs to limit traffic between critical systems.

4. Use Intrusion Detection Systems (IDS) for MITM Detection

Deploy SCADA-aware IDS tools like Snort, Zeek, or Suricata to detect suspicious traffic.

Set up log monitoring and alerts for unexpected changes in SCADA traffic.

5. Regularly Test for MITM Vulnerabilities

Conduct penetration testing to see how easily an attacker could insert themselves into SCADA traffic.

Simulate red team exercises to test network defenses against MITM attacks.

Final Thoughts: Defend the Grid, or Someone Else Will Control It

MITM attacks on SCADA systems aren't just theoretical—they're happening right now. Attackers don't need physical access to critical infrastructure if they can hijack network traffic remotely.

So the real question is: Do you want your power grid, water plant, or industrial facility to be controlled by you… or by some hacker halfway across the world?

Lock it down. Encrypt everything. Assume someone is always listening. Because in the world of SCADA security, they probably are. 🔒

5.4 Gaining Unauthorized Access to ICS Devices and HMIs

Picture this: You're at a theme park, staring at the control panel for a roller coaster. One button speeds it up, another slows it down, and a third stops it entirely. Now imagine if that control panel were accessible from the internet. Sounds ridiculous, right? Well, welcome to Industrial Control System (ICS) security, where hackers can sometimes access critical infrastructure with the same ease as ordering pizza online.

Human-Machine Interfaces (HMIs) and ICS devices weren't designed with cybersecurity in mind. Many still run default credentials, outdated software, or are directly exposed to the internet. This chapter is about how attackers break into these systems, why it's so easy, and most importantly—how to stop them before they turn your factory, power grid, or water plant into a hacker's playground.

5.4.1 How Attackers Gain Access to ICS Devices and HMIs

ICS systems were built for reliability, not security. That's why attackers don't need sophisticated zero-day exploits to break in. Most of the time, they just rely on carelessness, weak security configurations, or forgotten devices connected to the internet.

Here are some of the most common ways hackers break into ICS systems:

1. Default or Weak Credentials (The "Admin/Admin" Problem)

Let's be honest—changing default passwords is hard. And by "hard," I mean, apparently so difficult that entire power plants, oil refineries, and manufacturing facilities forget to do it. Attackers often:

Use manufacturer default credentials (e.g., admin/admin, root/root).

Try common passwords like 123456, password, or welcome1.

Use leaked credentials from previous breaches (because people love reusing passwords).

☠ Real-World Example:

A security researcher found that an HMI for a hydroelectric plant was online with the default password. If an attacker had logged in, they could have controlled water flow and turbine speed remotely.

2. Internet-Exposed ICS Systems (Shodan Says Hello!)

Many ICS devices are directly accessible on the internet, sometimes without authentication. Attackers can find them using:

Shodan, Censys, and ZoomEye (search engines for internet-connected devices).

Public ICS device lists from previous scans.

Misconfigured remote desktop services (RDP, VNC, or TeamViewer).

☠ Real-World Example:

In 2020, a hacker remotely accessed a Florida water treatment plant's SCADA system through a poorly secured remote desktop connection. They attempted to increase sodium hydroxide levels in the water supply, potentially poisoning thousands.

3. Exploiting Unpatched Vulnerabilities

Many ICS devices run outdated firmware with known security holes. Attackers can exploit:

Unpatched vulnerabilities in SCADA software (e.g., CVE-2021-12345 in an old Siemens PLC).

Insecure web-based HMIs that allow command injection.

Hardcoded backdoor accounts (yes, some vendors still leave these in).

☠ Real-World Example:

In 2017, a vulnerability in Schneider Electric's Triconex Safety System allowed hackers to reprogram industrial controllers, causing shutdowns at a petrochemical plant in Saudi Arabia.

4. Social Engineering and Phishing

Why hack a device when you can just trick an operator into giving you access? Attackers commonly:

Send phishing emails with malicious attachments that install malware on ICS workstations.

Pretend to be IT support, asking employees for their login credentials.

Drop infected USB drives near a facility, hoping someone plugs them in.

💀 Real-World Example:

In the Stuxnet attack on Iran's nuclear program, attackers used infected USB drives to spread malware into an air-gapped facility, ultimately damaging centrifuges.

5.4.2 What Happens When Attackers Get In?

Once inside an ICS network, attackers can:

1. Modify HMI Controls (Messing with the Operators)

An HMI is the main interface for controlling industrial processes. Attackers can:

Change setpoints (e.g., increasing boiler temperature until it explodes).

Falsify sensor readings (e.g., making an overloaded turbine appear fine).

Disable alarms, preventing operators from noticing problems.

💀 Scary Example:

An attacker hijacks an HMI for an oil pipeline, increases pressure beyond safe limits, and causes an explosion.

2. Deploy Ransomware (Holding Factories Hostage)

Many ransomware gangs now target ICS environments because downtime costs millions. Attacks often:

Lock operators out of HMIs and SCADA systems.

Demand ransom in Bitcoin to restore access.

Disrupt production at power plants, water facilities, and manufacturing plants.

💀 Real-World Example:

In 2021, the Colonial Pipeline ransomware attack led to fuel shortages across the U.S. because operators lost access to control systems.

3. Cause Physical Damage (Yes, Hackers Can Break Stuff!)

By manipulating PLCs and actuators, attackers can damage physical equipment. This is called a cyber-physical attack.

💀 Real-World Example:

In 2015, Russian hackers shut down parts of Ukraine's power grid, leaving 230,000 people without electricity.

5.4.3 How to Protect ICS Devices and HMIs from Hackers

1. Change Default Credentials (Seriously, Just Do It!)

Use strong, unique passwords for every ICS device.

Disable default accounts and backdoor credentials.

Enforce multi-factor authentication (MFA) for remote access.

2. Remove ICS Systems from the Internet

Use firewalls to block direct internet access.

Require VPNs and secure remote access solutions.

Regularly scan for exposed devices on Shodan.

3. Keep Software and Firmware Updated

Patch vulnerabilities in SCADA software, HMIs, and PLCs.

Disable unnecessary services and ports.

Use endpoint protection to detect malware.

4. Monitor for Intrusions and Anomalies

Deploy intrusion detection systems (IDS) that understand ICS traffic.

Enable logging and alerting on all critical devices.

Use behavioral analytics to detect unauthorized actions.

5. Train Employees to Recognize Phishing and Social Engineering

Conduct regular security awareness training.

Implement USB security policies (disable auto-run, scan all USBs).

Use security drills and red team exercises to test employee awareness.

Final Thoughts: If You Don't Secure Your ICS, Hackers Will Run Your Factory for You

Let's be real—attackers don't need fancy exploits if ICS devices are left wide open. Gaining unauthorized access to an HMI shouldn't be as easy as logging into Netflix, but in many cases, it is.

If you're in charge of securing ICS environments, don't wait for an attack to happen. Lock things down before some hacker in a basement (or a government-funded cyber warfare unit) decides to flip the wrong switch.

Because if they do, you won't be reading about it in a book—you'll be seeing it on the news. 📢

5.5 Defensive Strategies for Protecting SCADA Systems

If securing a Supervisory Control and Data Acquisition (SCADA) system were as easy as locking your front door, we wouldn't be seeing power grids getting hacked, water treatment plants being tampered with, and pipelines shutting down due to ransomware. But here we are.

SCADA systems weren't exactly designed with modern cybersecurity in mind. These networks run mission-critical infrastructure, often using decades-old software, weak authentication, and way too many internet-facing connections. But don't panic—this chapter is all about turning your SCADA fortress from a hacker's dream into an impenetrable nightmare for attackers.

5.5.1 Why SCADA Systems Are Hard to Secure

Before diving into defense strategies, let's address the elephant in the server room:

Legacy Systems: Many SCADA networks run on Windows XP (yes, really) or even custom-built hardware from the '90s that vendors stopped supporting long ago.

Availability Over Security: These systems are designed to run 24/7, meaning security patches are often delayed (or ignored) because downtime isn't an option.

Flat Networks: In many cases, everything is connected to everything, meaning once an attacker gets in, they can move freely across the network.

Internet Exposure: Thanks to remote access tools, cloud integration, and poor segmentation, SCADA networks are often reachable from the internet—sometimes without authentication.

Now, let's break down the must-have defensive strategies to keep attackers out.

5.5.2 Implementing Network Segmentation (Keep the Bad Guys Contained)

Imagine you live in a house where one key opens every door—if a burglar gets in, they have full access. That's how flat SCADA networks operate.

What to Do Instead:

Use the Purdue Model: Divide SCADA networks into zones (IT, DMZ, OT, and field devices) to restrict movement between layers.

Deploy Firewalls Between IT and OT Networks: Only allow necessary communication between corporate and SCADA environments.

Limit Remote Access: Instead of direct VPN access, use jump servers or remote desktop gateways with multi-factor authentication (MFA).

💀 **Worst-Case Scenario If You Ignore This:**

A hacker breaches an office workstation, moves laterally to the SCADA environment, and remotely shuts down an entire power grid (yes, this has actually happened).

5.5.3 Enforcing Strong Authentication (No More "Admin/Admin")

Too many SCADA systems still rely on:

Default credentials (seriously, change them).

Weak passwords (123456, password1, welcome123—you get the idea).

Shared accounts where everyone logs in as "Admin."

What to Do Instead:

Enforce Multi-Factor Authentication (MFA) for all remote and privileged accounts.

Disable Default Accounts and change all vendor-supplied credentials.

Use Role-Based Access Control (RBAC) to limit who can do what.

💀 **Worst-Case Scenario If You Ignore This:**

An attacker finds default credentials in a vendor manual, logs into an HMI, and manipulates water treatment chemicals remotely (yep, this actually happened in Florida).

5.5.4 Patching and Updating (Even If It's Painful)

SCADA operators hate patching. Why? Because downtime equals lost revenue, safety risks, and angry executives. Unfortunately, unpatched vulnerabilities are how hackers waltz into your system like they own the place.

What to Do Instead:

Prioritize Security Patches: Not every patch needs immediate installation, but critical vulnerabilities should be addressed ASAP.

Test Updates in a Lab Environment First: This prevents unexpected failures in production.

Use Virtual Patching: If patching a system isn't possible, use intrusion prevention systems (IPS) to block exploit attempts.

💀 **Worst-Case Scenario If You Ignore This:**

A known PLC vulnerability remains unpatched, allowing hackers to execute remote code and sabotage an industrial process (hello, Stuxnet).

5.5.5 Deploying Intrusion Detection and Monitoring (Because You Need to See the Attacks Coming)

Most SCADA breaches happen silently—operators only realize something's wrong after the damage is done.

What to Do Instead:

Use SCADA-Specific Intrusion Detection Systems (IDS) to spot unusual activity.

Enable Logging and Alerts on critical components (PLCs, HMIs, firewalls).

Implement Network Traffic Analysis (NTA) to detect unauthorized connections.

💀 **Worst-Case Scenario If You Ignore This:**

A hacker quietly monitors SCADA traffic for months, learning how your systems operate before launching a targeted attack that nobody sees coming.

5.5.6 Defending Against Ransomware (Because Downtime Is Expensive)

Ransomware attacks on SCADA systems aren't theoretical—they're already happening. Attackers know that disrupting critical infrastructure forces companies to pay up fast.

What to Do Instead:

Implement Offline Backups so recovery doesn't depend on paying ransom.

Use Application Whitelisting to prevent unauthorized software from running.

Regularly Test Incident Response Plans so operators know how to react.

💀 Worst-Case Scenario If You Ignore This:

A ransomware gang locks down an oil pipeline, demanding millions in Bitcoin while fuel shortages spread across the country (yes, Colonial Pipeline was just the beginning).

Final Thoughts: Make SCADA Security a Priority Before Hackers Make It One for You

Defending SCADA systems isn't optional anymore. Attackers are already targeting these networks, and it's only a matter of time before they find a way in—if they haven't already.

If you're managing SCADA security, take these defensive strategies seriously:

✓ Segment your network.

✓ Enforce strong authentication.

✓ Patch critical vulnerabilities.

✓ Monitor everything.

✓ Prepare for ransomware attacks.

Because if you don't, the first sign of a breach might be when your entire operation grinds to a halt. And trust me, explaining to your boss why the entire grid just went dark is a conversation you don't want to have. 🚨

Chapter 6: Wireless and RF Attacks on Smart Grid Infrastructure

Picture this: you're sipping your coffee, basking in the glow of your smart home, everything humming along as it should. The lights flicker on, the thermostat knows exactly how warm you like it, and you can even check on your power usage from your phone while lounging on the couch. But what if someone, sitting halfway across the world (or maybe just next door), was using those same wireless signals to mess with your grid? Sounds like something out of a spy thriller, right? Well, buckle up! Wireless and RF (radio frequency) attacks are a real-world threat to smart grid infrastructure, and it's time we dive into the world of invisible, but very real, cyber warfare that could send your electric system into chaos—no drama necessary.

In this chapter, we will explore the vulnerabilities introduced into the Smart Grid through wireless communication technologies, focusing on how malicious actors can exploit radio frequency (RF) signals to infiltrate critical infrastructure. These wireless communications play a pivotal role in the operation and management of smart grids, allowing for remote control and monitoring of power distribution networks. However, the very openness and convenience of these technologies also create significant security risks. We will analyze various types of RF and wireless attacks, examine case studies of real-world incidents, and discuss methods of mitigation to protect the integrity of the grid from unauthorized access, interference, and sabotage.

6.1 Exploiting Weaknesses in Smart Grid RF Communications

Let's be honest—when most people think about hacking, they picture a hoodie-wearing hacker furiously typing away in a dimly lit basement. But in the smart grid world, hacking can be as simple as sitting in a parked car with a laptop, a software-defined radio (SDR), and a good antenna.

Smart grid systems love wireless communication. Why? Because running cables everywhere is expensive and impractical. Instead, utilities rely on radio frequency (RF) technologies like Zigbee, LoRa, Wi-SUN, and even 5G to connect smart meters, substations, and other critical devices. The problem? RF signals don't have walls. Anyone with the right gear can eavesdrop, intercept, or even hijack these signals from a distance.

So, let's break down exactly how RF attacks work and why your neighbor's teenage hacker son might be more dangerous to your electricity bill than you think.

6.1.1 Why RF Communications Are Vulnerable

Unlike traditional network hacking, where an attacker needs a physical or logical connection, RF hacking just requires a receiver and proximity—which can mean sitting outside a substation or even flying a drone near critical infrastructure.

Here's why RF communications in the smart grid are an attractive target for attackers:

Broadcast Nature: RF signals travel in all directions, making interception easy.

Lack of Encryption: Many legacy smart grid RF protocols either don't encrypt data or use weak encryption that can be cracked.

Weak Authentication: Some devices rely on static keys or no authentication at all, meaning an attacker can easily inject malicious commands.

Replay Attacks: RF protocols without proper security measures are vulnerable to record-and-replay attacks, where an attacker captures a valid transmission and replays it later to manipulate systems.

Now, let's talk about how attackers actually exploit these weaknesses.

6.1.2 Sniffing Smart Grid RF Traffic

Ever heard of RF sniffing? It's basically Wireshark for the airwaves. Attackers use devices like:

Software-Defined Radios (SDRs) (HackRF, RTL-SDR, BladeRF)

Zigbee Sniffers (TI CC2531, RZUSBstick)

LoRaWAN Sniffers (SX1276-based boards)

With the right gear, an attacker can capture unencrypted transmissions between smart meters, grid controllers, and substations. If those signals contain sensitive grid commands, meter readings, or authentication tokens, the attacker can then reverse-engineer the protocol and plan their next move.

💀 **Real-World Danger**: A researcher once used an SDR to intercept smart meter transmissions, allowing them to monitor and even manipulate energy consumption data.

6.1.3 Replay and Injection Attacks (Because Repeating Is Easy)

If a smart meter sends a command like "disconnect power", and the system doesn't require strong authentication, an attacker could capture that command and replay it later—turning off the power to any home or business they choose.

How Attackers Pull This Off:

Sniff the RF signal from a legitimate smart grid device.

Record the command (e.g., turning power off/on).

Replay it later, tricking the system into executing the command.

If the protocol lacks proper security mechanisms, the grid won't know the difference between a real operator and an attacker sitting in a car down the street.

💀 **Real-World Danger**: Researchers have demonstrated how Zigbee-based smart meters can be manipulated via replay attacks to cause billing fraud or even create blackout scenarios.

6.1.4 Jamming Attacks (When RF Becomes White Noise)

Unlike sniffing and replay attacks, RF jamming is brute force. Instead of trying to read or modify signals, an attacker simply floods the frequency band with interference, making communication impossible.

Common RF Jamming Techniques:

Broadband Jamming: Overloading an entire frequency range, knocking out all devices.

Targeted Jamming: Attacking only specific frequencies used by smart meters or control systems.

Reactive Jamming: Waiting for legitimate signals to appear and then immediately disrupting them.

Since many smart grid systems depend on uninterrupted RF communication, jamming attacks can cause:

Delayed or lost smart meter readings.

Loss of remote control over grid infrastructure.

Denial of service to energy management systems.

☠ **Real-World Danger**: A hacker with a $30 jammer could disable communication between thousands of smart meters, forcing utility companies to fall back on manual operations (which they're often not prepared for).

6.1.5 Attacking Zigbee, LoRa, and 5G-Based Smart Grid Systems

Zigbee (Popular, But Vulnerable)

Used in smart meters, home energy systems, and substation monitoring.

Known vulnerabilities include weak encryption and default keys.

Easily hacked with tools like KillerBee and the CC2531 sniffer.

LoRa (Long Range, Weak Security)

Often deployed in wide-area energy monitoring systems.

Vulnerable to packet sniffing and replay attacks.

Attackers can impersonate devices if encryption isn't enabled.

5G (Powerful, But Not Perfect)

Used for high-speed, low-latency smart grid operations.

Still susceptible to downgrade attacks, SS7 exploits, and fake base stations.

☠ **Real-World Danger**: A penetration test revealed that many LoRaWAN-based smart meters transmit authentication keys in plaintext, meaning anyone with a receiver can hijack the network.

6.1.6 Defending Against RF Attacks (Because You Don't Want a Blackout)

Now that we know how scarily vulnerable RF communications are, how do we secure them?

✅ **Use Strong Encryption:**

AES-128 or higher should be standard for all smart grid RF transmissions.

Avoid default or hardcoded encryption keys.

✅ **Implement Frequency Hopping:**

Spread spectrum techniques make it harder for attackers to jam signals.

Technologies like FHSS (Frequency Hopping Spread Spectrum) can mitigate targeted attacks.

✅ **Authenticate All Devices:**

Require mutual authentication between meters, controllers, and substations.

Use cryptographic signing to prevent spoofed commands.

✅ **Detect and Respond to RF Anomalies:**

Deploy RF intrusion detection systems (RF-IDS) to spot unauthorized transmissions.

Log and monitor signal disruptions to detect jamming attempts early.

Final Thoughts: The Smart Grid Needs Smarter Security

RF attacks on the smart grid aren't just theoretical—they're already happening. Whether it's sniffing unencrypted signals, replaying malicious commands, or jamming critical communications, attackers have plenty of ways to exploit weaknesses.

The best defense? Assume the airwaves aren't safe. Encrypt everything, authenticate every device, and monitor RF activity like your grid depends on it—because it does.

And if you're still not convinced, just remember: somewhere, right now, a hacker with an SDR is scanning the airwaves, looking for their next target. 📷

6.2 Sniffing and Intercepting Wireless Smart Meter Traffic

Let's play a game. Imagine you're a hacker, sitting comfortably in your car with a laptop, a software-defined radio (SDR), and a big cup of coffee. You turn on your SDR, fire up a packet sniffer, and within minutes, you're swimming in wireless smart meter data. Congratulations! You just intercepted someone's electricity usage, maybe even their account details. Welcome to the dark (but educational) side of RF hacking.

Smart meters are everywhere, and they talk wirelessly—to each other, to the grid, and sometimes even to whoever is listening. If they're not properly secured (spoiler: many aren't), attackers can eavesdrop on communications, steal private data, or even manipulate energy consumption records. In this chapter, we'll explore how hackers sniff and intercept wireless smart meter traffic, what kind of data they can extract, and most importantly—how to defend against these attacks.

6.2.1 How Smart Meters Communicate Wirelessly

Before we can hack smart meters (or defend them), we need to understand how they talk. Smart meters typically communicate using:

Zigbee – The most common protocol for home energy monitoring.

LoRaWAN – Used for long-range smart meter networks.

Wi-SUN – A mesh network technology used by some utilities.

Cellular (4G/5G) – Used for more advanced smart grid infrastructure.

PLC (Power Line Communication) – Okay, not wireless, but still worth mentioning.

Each of these technologies has strengths and weaknesses, but they all share one critical problem: they're transmitting data into the air, and anything transmitted can be intercepted.

6.2.2 Tools of the Trade: What Attackers Use to Sniff Smart Meter Traffic

Want to listen in on smart meter traffic? You don't need a spy van or a Hollywood hacking montage—you just need cheap, off-the-shelf hardware. Here's what attackers use:

1. Software-Defined Radios (SDRs)

HackRF One – Can listen to a wide range of frequencies, making it ideal for Zigbee, LoRa, and other protocols.

RTL-SDR – A cheaper option, great for basic RF monitoring.

BladeRF or LimeSDR – Advanced options with better sensitivity.

2. Zigbee and LoRa Sniffers

Texas Instruments CC2531 – A USB stick that can capture Zigbee packets like a charm.

SX1276 LoRa Module – Used to intercept long-range smart meter signals.

3. RF Analysis Software

Wireshark + Zigbee Plugin – Helps decode and analyze Zigbee smart meter packets.

GQRX & SDR# – Used for signal discovery and real-time RF monitoring.

URH (Universal Radio Hacker) – One of the best tools for analyzing and replaying RF traffic.

💀 **Real-World Scenario**: A security researcher once used a simple RTL-SDR and a Zigbee sniffer to intercept smart meter traffic from an entire neighborhood, revealing usage patterns and even customer IDs.

6.2.3 What Attackers Can See in Sniffed Smart Meter Data

So, what kind of juicy information can a hacker get by sniffing smart meter traffic? Plenty! Here are some of the most common data leaks:

Energy Consumption Data – Want to know when someone is home? Just check their smart meter readings.

Billing Information – Some meters transmit account details in plaintext (yes, really).

Meter Commands – In poorly secured networks, commands like disconnect/reconnect power can be intercepted and replayed.

Encryption Keys or Tokens – If not implemented properly, an attacker can grab authentication keys and gain full control over a meter.

💀 **Real-World Scenario**: In one penetration test, researchers intercepted unencrypted Zigbee commands that allowed them to remotely disable smart meters without authentication.

6.2.4 Replay and Injection Attacks on Smart Meters

Let's say an attacker captures a command like "shut down power to Meter #1234." If the system doesn't have proper security, the attacker can replay that exact command, effectively turning off power to any meter they want.

How Attackers Perform Replay Attacks:

Capture a legitimate command (e.g., power off, tariff change).

Analyze the protocol to understand how commands are structured.

Resend the same packet to trick the meter into executing the command again.

💀 **Real-World Scenario**: In a controlled lab test, security researchers replayed an "increase energy usage" command, making a meter report higher than actual consumption—leading to fraudulent overbilling.

6.2.5 Defending Against Smart Meter Sniffing Attacks

The good news? There are ways to prevent attackers from listening in on smart meter communications. The bad news? Many utilities still don't implement these protections properly.

✅ Use Strong Encryption

All smart meter communications should use AES-128 or AES-256 encryption.

Avoid using default or hardcoded keys (yes, some still do this ☐).

✅ Implement Secure Authentication

Use mutual authentication so both meters and the grid verify each other before exchanging data.

Rotate authentication keys frequently to prevent replay attacks.

✅ Use Frequency Hopping & Spread Spectrum Techniques

FHSS (Frequency Hopping Spread Spectrum) makes it harder for attackers to sniff continuous data streams.

LoRaWAN Adaptive Data Rate (ADR) can make sniffing harder by changing signal parameters dynamically.

✅ Detect and Respond to RF Anomalies

Deploy RF Intrusion Detection Systems (RF-IDS) to monitor for unauthorized signals.

Set up anomaly detection to spot unusual energy usage or unauthorized meter commands.

💡 **Pro Tip**: Security isn't just about making attacks impossible—it's about making attacks so difficult that hackers move on to an easier target.

Final Thoughts: Protecting the Smart Grid from RF Eavesdroppers

Sniffing smart meter traffic is easier than you'd think—and the consequences range from privacy violations to full-blown energy fraud. The solution? Encrypt everything, authenticate every device, and monitor your RF spectrum like your grid depends on it—because it does.

And if you're a utility company still running unencrypted Zigbee meters... well, let's just say, you should probably fix that before someone else does. 😺

6.3 Replay and Jamming Attacks on Zigbee and LoRa-Based Devices

Let's start with a little thought experiment. Imagine you're a hacker (for educational purposes, of course). You're sitting in a coffee shop, laptop open, a small software-defined radio (SDR) device plugged in, and a mischievous grin on your face. You send a single command over the air—lights off. Suddenly, an entire block goes dark. No, you're not a magician. You've just executed a replay attack on a poorly secured Zigbee-based smart grid system.

Or maybe you're in your car, parked outside a house, and you fire up a radio jammer. Within seconds, every Zigbee-based smart meter in the area stops communicating with the grid. Congratulations, you've just jammed an entire neighborhood's energy monitoring system. Who knew cybercrime could be this easy? (Don't actually do this.)

Now, before any real hackers get excited—let's talk about what these attacks are, why they work, and most importantly, how to defend against them.

6.3.1 Understanding Replay and Jamming Attacks

Both replay and jamming attacks target the wireless communication channels of smart grid devices, particularly those using Zigbee and LoRa protocols.

☐ Replay Attacks: What They Are and How They Work

A replay attack is like stealing someone's garage door opener signal and using it to open their door later. It works like this:

Intercept a valid command (e.g., "turn off smart meter," "change energy tariff").

Record the command using an SDR, Zigbee sniffer, or LoRa receiver.

Resend the exact same command at a later time to trick the system into executing it again.

💀 **Example Attack**: A hacker captures a "disconnect power" command sent to a Zigbee-based smart meter. Later, they replay that command, cutting off power to the meter—without authentication.

📢 **Jamming Attacks: The Digital Silence Button**

Jamming attacks are even simpler. Instead of replaying a signal, the attacker just floods the airwaves with noise, making it impossible for devices to communicate.

Zigbee Jamming – Attackers can use a cheap 2.4 GHz jammer to block smart meter signals.

LoRa Jamming – Since LoRa operates in sub-GHz frequencies, attackers need an SDR that can generate noise in those bands.

💀 **Example Attack**: A hacker parks near a substation, activates a LoRa jammer, and disrupts the communication between smart meters and the utility grid, preventing data collection.

6.3.2 Why Zigbee and LoRa Are Vulnerable

Smart grid devices use low-power, long-range, and low-bandwidth wireless communication—great for efficiency, bad for security. Here's why they're vulnerable:

Zigbee Weaknesses

Uses 2.4 GHz, which is easily jammed by Wi-Fi interference.

Many devices use default network keys, making them easy to intercept and exploit.

Some Zigbee devices lack replay protection, allowing attackers to resend old commands.

LoRa Weaknesses

LoRaWAN packets can be sniffed and replayed if encryption isn't properly implemented.

LoRa networks operate on unlicensed frequencies, making them easy to jam.

Some LoRa deployments lack device authentication, allowing attackers to inject malicious packets.

💀 **Real-World Example**: Researchers have successfully performed LoRa replay attacks to falsify smart meter readings, tricking utility companies into reporting incorrect power usage.

6.3.3 Tools Attackers Use for Replay and Jamming Attacks

A hacker doesn't need expensive equipment to exploit Zigbee or LoRa devices. Here are the go-to tools for these attacks:

Replay Attack Tools

Texas Instruments CC2531 – A cheap USB Zigbee sniffer that can capture and replay packets.

HackRF One – An SDR that can record and replay both Zigbee and LoRa signals.

LoRaWAN Sniffer (SX1276-based) – Used to capture and manipulate LoRa traffic.

Jamming Attack Tools

Simple 2.4 GHz RF Jammer – Blocks Zigbee signals with basic RF noise.

HackRF One + GNU Radio – Can generate wideband noise to jam LoRa and Zigbee.

ESP8266 Deauther – While mainly used for Wi-Fi deauthentication, can be modified for Zigbee jamming.

💀 **Real-World Example**: Security researchers demonstrated a Zigbee jamming attack that disabled an entire smart home using a $10 RF jammer.

6.3.4 Defending Against Replay and Jamming Attacks

Now that we've seen how bad things can get, how do we fix this?

✅ Preventing Replay Attacks

Use Nonces and Timestamps – Every wireless packet should have a unique nonce or timestamp to prevent replaying old commands.

Implement Message Authentication Codes (MACs) – Helps detect if a packet has been tampered with.

Use Strong Encryption (AES-128 or AES-256) – Prevents attackers from easily modifying packets.

Enable Challenge-Response Authentication – Forces the system to verify every command before execution.

💡 **Best Practice**: If a smart meter receives a command identical to a previous one without a fresh authentication token, it should reject it.

✅ Preventing Jamming Attacks

Use Frequency Hopping Spread Spectrum (FHSS) – Continuously switches frequencies, making it harder for jammers to block signals.

Increase Transmission Power – Stronger signals are harder to jam.

Deploy Redundant Communication Channels – If Zigbee is jammed, fall back to cellular or PLC.

Monitor for RF Interference – Deploy RF intrusion detection systems (RF-IDS) to detect jamming attempts.

💡 **Best Practice**: Implement automatic failover mechanisms so that if a LoRa or Zigbee signal is disrupted, the system can switch to a backup communication channel.

Final Thoughts: Secure Your Smart Grid Before Hackers Do

The scary part? Replay and jamming attacks are ridiculously easy to pull off. The good news? With proper security measures—strong encryption, authentication, and frequency hopping—you can make these attacks a nightmare for any hacker.

So, if you're designing or deploying smart grid devices, take security seriously. Because if you don't, some bored hacker with a $30 SDR and too much free time will. 😼

6.4 Exploiting Vulnerabilities in 5G and Cellular IoT (CIoT) Smart Grid Systems

Let's start with a simple question: What happens when you combine the power of 5G with a critical infrastructure like the smart grid?

Well, in theory, you get faster, more reliable, and more scalable energy networks that can handle everything from smart meters to automated substations. But in practice? You also get a hacker's playground.

5G and Cellular IoT (CIoT) promise ultra-low latency, massive connectivity, and real-time smart grid automation. But these networks also introduce new attack surfaces, legacy security gaps, and vulnerabilities that cybercriminals can exploit. And trust me—hackers love playing with new toys.

So, let's break down how attackers can target 5G-enabled smart grids and what we can do to stop them before they turn out the lights.

6.4.1 The Role of 5G and CIoT in Smart Grid Systems

To understand the security risks, we first need to understand how 5G and Cellular IoT (CIoT) fit into the modern smart grid.

⚡ 5G in Smart Grid Networks

5G offers high-speed, low-latency communication, making it perfect for:

Real-time grid monitoring and automation

Connecting millions of IoT sensors and smart meters

Enabling AI-driven energy management

Supporting Vehicle-to-Grid (V2G) communication for EVs

🐉 Cellular IoT (CIoT) in Smart Grids

CIoT, including NB-IoT (Narrowband IoT) and LTE-M, enables:

Long-range, low-power connectivity for smart meters

Remote control of distributed energy resources (DERs)

Data transmission from edge devices with minimal bandwidth

Sounds great, right? Not so fast.

While 5G and CIoT improve efficiency, they also expand the attack surface—creating new vulnerabilities that hackers are already exploring.

6.4.2 Attack Surfaces in 5G and CIoT Smart Grids

🚀 Network Slicing Attacks

5G introduces a concept called network slicing, which allows utilities to create dedicated virtual networks for different applications. While this improves efficiency, it also:

Creates isolated attack vectors—if an attacker compromises one slice, they could jump to another.

Lacks proper isolation—poorly implemented security controls may allow lateral movement between slices.

💀 **Example Attack**: A hacker compromises a 5G smart meter slice, then moves laterally to a higher-privileged substation control slice, gaining control over energy distribution.

📶 Man-in-the-Middle (MITM) Attacks on 5G Smart Grid Devices

Since 5G uses cellular towers to relay smart grid data, attackers can set up a rogue 5G base station to intercept and modify smart grid communications.

💀 **Example Attack:**

A hacker deploys a fake 5G tower near a power plant.

Smart grid devices connect to it, thinking it's legitimate.

The attacker alters energy consumption data, leading to incorrect billing or grid instability.

🏴 Jamming and Denial-of-Service (DoS) on 5G and CIoT

Unlike wired networks, wireless networks are always susceptible to jamming.

5G uses millimeter-wave frequencies, which can be disrupted with targeted interference.

CIoT relies on low-power LTE-M and NB-IoT, making it vulnerable to wideband jamming.

💀 **Example Attack**: A hacker with a cheap SDR and a power amplifier jams 5G communication between grid substations, delaying critical power adjustments and causing blackouts.

☐ SIM Card Exploits and Subscriber Identity Theft

Smart grid devices using eSIMs or physical SIMs for CIoT connectivity can be:

Cloned (attackers duplicate SIM credentials).

Hijacked (attackers redirect traffic from smart grid devices to rogue servers).

Brute-forced (weak authentication methods allow SIM identity theft).

💀 **Example Attack**: A hacker steals SIM credentials from an NB-IoT smart meter and redirects billing data, making it look like someone else is using all the electricity.

☐ Lack of End-to-End Encryption in CIoT Data Transmission

Many IoT devices still transmit data in plaintext or use weak encryption like TLS 1.0—which can be broken.

💀 **Example Attack:**

A hacker intercepts unencrypted CIoT smart meter data.

They modify consumption reports to lower their energy bills or cause inaccurate demand forecasting.

6.4.3 Exploit Tools for 5G and CIoT Smart Grid Attacks

Now that we know the weaknesses, let's talk about the tools hackers use to exploit them.

☐ Tools for Network Slicing and MITM Attacks

Open5GS – Open-source 5G core network for testing slicing vulnerabilities.

srsRAN (formerly srsLTE) – Used for setting up rogue 5G base stations.

IMSI Catchers (Stingrays) – Used to intercept and spoof cellular connections.

📡 Tools for Jamming and Denial-of-Service

HackRF One – Can be used to jam 5G and NB-IoT signals.

BladeRF – A powerful SDR for millimeter-wave jamming.

RF Power Amplifiers – Boost interference signals to disrupt cellular communication.

📡 Tools for SIM Exploits and IoT Device Hacking

Osmocom SIMtrace – Can be used to sniff, clone, or intercept SIM card traffic.

Modmproxy + Wireshark – Can be used to sniff and manipulate unencrypted CIoT traffic.

6.4.4 Securing 5G and CIoT Smart Grid Systems

Alright, enough doom and gloom. How do we defend against these attacks?

✓ Protecting Against Network Slicing Attacks

Implement strict access controls between slices.

Use Zero Trust Architecture (ZTA) to prevent lateral movement.

Continuously monitor for unauthorized slice access attempts.

✅ Preventing MITM and Rogue Base Station Attacks

Enable mutual authentication between smart grid devices and 5G networks.

Use strong cryptographic protocols like TLS 1.3 or IPsec.

Deploy cellular anomaly detection systems to detect rogue towers.

✅ Defending Against Jamming and DoS Attacks

Use frequency-hopping techniques to make jamming more difficult.

Deploy backup communication channels (satellite, fiber, or PLC).

Monitor RF spectrum activity for abnormal interference.

✅ Hardening SIM Security in CIoT Devices

Implement eSIM technology with remote authentication to prevent cloning.

Use SIM-based authentication combined with additional security layers.

Monitor SIM usage patterns for suspicious activity.

Final Thoughts: 5G and CIoT Security Must Be a Priority

5G and CIoT are revolutionizing the smart grid—but if we don't secure them properly, they'll become a hacker's dream come true.

As we adopt these new technologies, we must think like attackers to build resilient, secure smart grids. Because let's be real—if you don't secure your 5G-enabled smart grid, someone with a $100 SDR and a bad attitude will. 😼

6.5 Defending Wireless Smart Grid Networks Against Cyber Attacks

Alright, let's get real for a second. Wireless networks are amazing—no messy cables, no digging trenches, and no physical break-ins required for an attacker to wreak havoc. Sounds great, right? Well, it's also a nightmare for cybersecurity.

Smart grid networks rely on wireless technologies like LoRa, Zigbee, Wi-SUN, 5G, and Cellular IoT to connect smart meters, substations, and distributed energy resources. But here's the catch: hackers love wireless systems because they can attack from a distance. Why physically break into a substation when you can just sit in a car with a laptop and an SDR (Software-Defined Radio) and start messing with the grid?

So, the real question is: how do we defend wireless smart grid networks against these threats? Buckle up, because we're about to break it all down.

6.5.1 Understanding Wireless Threats in Smart Grid Networks

Before we dive into defense strategies, let's go over the main ways hackers attack wireless smart grids:

📡 Eavesdropping on Unencrypted Communications

Attackers sniff smart grid traffic to gather intelligence.

If data is sent in plaintext, they can steal information, manipulate energy readings, or reverse-engineer commands.

📢 Jamming Attacks and Denial-of-Service (DoS)

Hackers flood the network with noise to disrupt communications.

Jamming can prevent critical grid control commands from reaching substations, leading to power disruptions.

🔁 Replay and Spoofing Attacks

Attackers capture and replay legitimate signals, fooling smart grid devices into executing malicious commands.

Spoofing allows them to impersonate smart meters, substations, or control systems.

🎭 Man-in-the-Middle (MITM) Attacks

Hackers intercept and alter smart grid data in transit.

This can lead to false power demand readings, remote manipulation of devices, or unauthorized access.

6.5.2 Securing Smart Grid Wireless Communications

🔒 Encrypt Everything, Always

One of the biggest mistakes in IoT security is forgetting to encrypt data.

Use AES-256 encryption for LoRa, Zigbee, and Wi-SUN communications.

Implement TLS 1.3/IPsec for 5G and Cellular IoT (CIoT) traffic.

Never transmit plaintext credentials, commands, or meter readings.

✅ **Defense Tip**: Even if a hacker intercepts the data, strong encryption ensures they can't read or manipulate it.

📶 Protect Against Jamming Attacks

Wireless signals can be jammed, but we can make it harder for attackers.

Frequency Hopping Spread Spectrum (FHSS): Devices switch between frequencies, making jamming more difficult.

Adaptive Power Control: Dynamically adjust power levels to counteract interference.

Directional Antennas: Reduce exposure to external interference by focusing signal transmission.

✅ **Defense Tip**: Deploy backup wired or fiber connections for critical systems in case of jamming.

📡 Detect and Block Rogue Devices

Attackers love setting up fake smart meters, rogue access points, and malicious gateways.

Use Intrusion Detection Systems (IDS) to spot unauthorized devices.

Deploy device authentication using digital certificates (PKI).

Enable MAC address whitelisting to prevent unauthorized devices from connecting.

☑ **Defense Tip**: Continuously scan for unauthorized RF signals in smart grid environments.

🔑 Secure Wireless Protocols

Many wireless protocols used in the smart grid are insecure by default—but we can fix that.

LoRaWAN: Enable AES encryption and device authentication.

Zigbee: Use Zigbee 3.0 security features like link-layer encryption.

Wi-SUN: Implement message integrity verification to prevent tampering.

5G/CIoT: Use mutual authentication between devices and the network.

☑ **Defense Tip**: Regularly update firmware and security configurations to patch protocol vulnerabilities.

🔲🔲 Detect and Prevent MITM Attacks

Man-in-the-Middle attacks can be devastating, but we can make them nearly impossible.

Mutual authentication: Both endpoints must verify each other before exchanging data.

HMAC (Hash-based Message Authentication Code): Ensures data integrity and authenticity.

Anti-replay protections: Use timestamps and sequence numbers to prevent replay attacks.

☑ **Defense Tip**: Implement end-to-end encryption so that even if traffic is intercepted, it's useless to the attacker.

6.5.3 Physical Security Measures for Wireless Smart Grid Networks

Let's not forget: if an attacker can physically access your smart grid devices, it's game over.

☐ Harden Smart Meters and Wireless Devices

Tamper-resistant enclosures to prevent hardware manipulation.

Secure boot and firmware signing to prevent unauthorized firmware changes.

Disable unnecessary wireless interfaces to reduce attack vectors.

✓ **Defense Tip**: Conduct regular penetration testing to find and fix vulnerabilities before hackers do.

🔍 Continuous Monitoring and Threat Detection

The best defense is knowing when something suspicious is happening.

Deploy SIEM (Security Information and Event Management) systems to detect anomalies.

Use AI-driven anomaly detection to identify unusual traffic patterns.

Monitor RF spectrum activity to detect jamming or unauthorized transmissions.

✓ **Defense Tip**: Set up real-time alerts for any suspicious activity in your smart grid network.

6.5.4 Future-Proofing Wireless Smart Grid Security

Technology evolves, and so do cyber threats. How do we stay ahead?

🚀 Moving Towards Zero Trust Architecture (ZTA)

Never assume any device or connection is safe.

Continuous authentication and least-privilege access for smart grid components.

Segment networks so that a compromised device can't affect the entire grid.

☐ Leveraging AI and Machine Learning for Security

AI-driven security can:

Detect anomalous behavior in smart grid traffic.

Identify potential attack patterns before they escalate.

Automate real-time security responses to threats.

Final Thoughts: Staying Ahead of Wireless Cyber Threats

Wireless smart grid networks are convenient, scalable, and efficient—but also vulnerable to cyber attacks if not secured properly.

By implementing strong encryption, intrusion detection, protocol hardening, and AI-driven monitoring, we can protect our energy infrastructure from cyber threats.

Because let's be honest—losing Wi-Fi is annoying, but losing power? That's a disaster. Let's keep the lights on and the hackers out. 💡🔒📡

Chapter 7: Attacking Grid Edge Computing and IoT Devices

Imagine you're at the cutting edge of technology: self-driving cars zipping by, drones delivering your packages, and your smart refrigerator telling you when you're out of milk— all thanks to the wonders of the Internet of Things (IoT). Now, let's toss in the fact that the same tech powers the Smart Grid, with edge computing sitting pretty at the heart of it all, helping manage everything from sensors to remote meters. Sounds pretty awesome, right? But wait... what if someone figures out how to hack into that grid edge, turning your smart home into a hacker's playground? Edge computing and IoT devices make life easier, but they also open the door to some serious cyber shenanigans. In this chapter, we'll take a deep dive into how attackers are zeroing in on the very devices that make our grids "smart," and how it can all go horribly wrong. Buckle up for a thrilling ride through the vulnerabilities lurking just a click (or hack) away.

This chapter provides a thorough examination of the security challenges associated with grid edge computing and IoT devices within the smart grid framework. As edge computing becomes increasingly integrated into power distribution systems, it enables real-time processing and decision-making at the edge of the network, reducing latency and improving efficiency. However, the proliferation of IoT devices—ranging from sensors to smart meters—creates a wide attack surface for cyber threats. We will explore various techniques used by attackers to compromise these devices, from exploiting weak authentication mechanisms to launching distributed denial-of-service (DDoS) attacks. Furthermore, we will discuss effective countermeasures and strategies to secure grid edge computing and IoT devices, ensuring that they continue to serve their intended purpose without exposing critical infrastructure to undue risks.

7.1 Understanding Grid Edge Computing and Decentralized Energy Systems

Alright, let's start with the fun part—imagine you're hosting a party, and suddenly, everyone decides they need to charge their phones at the same time. The power strip is overloaded, your circuit breaker trips, and boom—party's over. ☐💡 Now, imagine that happening on a city-wide scale with thousands of electric vehicles (EVs), rooftop solar panels, and smart devices pulling power from the grid at random. Sounds chaotic, right? That's where grid edge computing comes in.

Grid edge computing is the smart grid's way of saying, "Hey, let's not send all decisions to some big central system. Let's be smarter and handle things closer to where they happen." It distributes computing power to the "edge" of the network—near smart meters, substations, EV chargers, and distributed energy resources (DERs) like wind turbines and battery storage. This approach reduces latency, improves efficiency, and enhances security (or at least, that's the goal… until hackers come knocking).

What is Grid Edge Computing?

Grid edge computing is all about processing data where it's generated, rather than sending everything to a central data center. It relies on IoT devices, AI-driven analytics, and localized decision-making to optimize energy distribution in real time.

Key Characteristics of Grid Edge Computing:

Decentralized Processing: Devices like smart inverters and grid controllers make independent decisions.

Real-Time Responsiveness: Fast adjustments to power supply and demand fluctuations.

Energy Efficiency: Reduces strain on central grid infrastructure and improves reliability.

Improved Security: Less reliance on a single control point, reducing the risk of catastrophic failure.

This is crucial because modern energy grids aren't just one-way power highways anymore. Instead of just sending electricity from big power plants to homes, we now have two-way energy flow—where homes with solar panels, battery storage, and EVs can also send power back to the grid. This shift is what makes decentralized energy systems both exciting and challenging.

The Role of Decentralized Energy Systems

A decentralized energy system isn't some sci-fi concept—it's happening right now. Cities and businesses are moving away from centralized fossil-fuel-based power generation and adopting local energy sources like:

Solar farms ☀☐

Wind turbines ☐

Battery storage systems 🔋

Microgrids & Virtual Power Plants (VPPs) ☐

Unlike traditional grids, which are top-down systems, decentralized grids are more like a swarm of intelligent, self-sustaining energy nodes. These systems rely on machine learning algorithms, predictive analytics, and automated control mechanisms to keep everything balanced.

Why is Grid Edge Computing Critical for the Future?

If you've ever experienced a blackout, you know how frustrating it is. Now imagine a grid that anticipates power failures and reroutes energy automatically before you even notice. That's the magic of grid edge computing.

Here's why it's a game-changer:

Increased Grid Resilience ☐

Decentralized energy resources reduce the impact of outages.

Microgrids can operate independently when the main grid fails.

Lower Latency in Energy Management ⚡

Critical decisions (like load balancing) happen at the edge, not in a far-away control center.

Real-time data processing allows faster response to demand spikes.

Cost Savings for Utilities and Consumers 💰

Smarter energy distribution means less wasted electricity.

Consumers can participate in demand response programs to save money.

Better Integration of Renewable Energy 🌱

AI-driven edge computing helps manage variable power sources like wind and solar.

Smart systems optimize energy storage and distribution dynamically.

The Security Challenges of Grid Edge Computing

Now for the not-so-fun part—grid edge computing introduces new attack surfaces that hackers love to exploit. Since we now have millions of connected IoT devices making energy decisions, security risks are through the roof.

Cybersecurity Risks at the Edge

Unprotected IoT Devices: Many grid-edge devices lack basic security protections (like strong authentication).

Data Manipulation Attacks: Attackers could alter grid sensor data to cause power instability.

Compromised Edge Nodes: If a single node is hacked, it can spread malware across the grid.

Denial-of-Service (DoS) Attacks: Attackers could overload edge computing nodes, disrupting energy flow.

✅ **Solution**: Implement Zero Trust Architecture (ZTA), where every device must authenticate before accessing grid resources.

Final Thoughts: The Future of Grid Edge Computing

Grid edge computing is revolutionizing how we generate, distribute, and consume electricity. It's paving the way for a more efficient, resilient, and sustainable energy grid—but only if we secure it properly.

So next time you charge your EV, turn on your solar-powered AC, or plug in your smart toaster, remember: somewhere at the edge of the grid, a tiny computer is working hard to keep the lights on—just make sure hackers don't take control of it first. 🔋⚡

7.2 Exploiting Edge Devices and Gateway Vulnerabilities

Alright, let's talk about hacking the edge of the grid—the place where smart meters, sensors, EV chargers, and IoT gateways all come together in a beautiful, chaotic mess of connected devices. If smart grids were a medieval castle, edge devices would be the poorly guarded side doors that hackers just love sneaking through.

See, the energy industry got excited about edge computing because it makes power distribution smarter and more efficient. But guess what? More intelligence means more attack surfaces. And if there's one thing we know about cybercriminals, it's that they love a good vulnerability. So, let's dive into how attackers exploit edge devices and gateways, and why securing them is more critical than ever.

What Are Edge Devices and Gateways in the Smart Grid?

Before we break into them (metaphorically speaking, of course), let's define what we're dealing with:

Edge Devices

These are the frontline gadgets of the smart grid. They gather, process, and send data to the cloud or control center. Some common examples include:

Smart meters (measure power usage)

Grid sensors (monitor voltage, frequency, etc.)

EV charging stations (manage energy flow to cars)

Distributed Energy Resource (DER) **controllers** (control solar, wind, and batteries)

Gateways

Think of gateways as traffic cops. They manage communications between edge devices and the broader smart grid network. Examples include:

IoT gateways (translate protocols between devices)

Substation routers (secure communication hubs for power substations)

Energy management systems (EMS) (coordinate data from multiple devices)

Now, if these devices were properly secured, we wouldn't have much to talk about. But let's be real—many of them are not.

How Hackers Exploit Edge Devices and Gateways

Edge devices and gateways sit at the intersection of IT and OT (Operational Technology), making them juicy targets. Here's how attackers break in:

1. Weak Authentication & Default Credentials

Many edge devices still ship with factory-set passwords like "admin/admin" or "1234" (yes, in 2025, this is still a thing). Attackers can:

✅ Use Shodan or Censys to find exposed smart meters and gateways.

✅ Try default or weak credentials.

✅ Gain access and pivot deeper into the grid.

🔥 **Real-world Example**: In 2019, hackers accessed thousands of industrial IoT devices due to default passwords. No hacking tools required—just Google and a little patience.

2. Unpatched Firmware & Outdated Software

Let's face it—nobody likes updating firmware. But when you ignore updates, you're basically putting a neon sign on your device that says, "Hack me, please!"

Attackers can:

✅ Exploit known CVE vulnerabilities in outdated firmware.

✅ Use buffer overflow attacks to take over the device.

✅ Deploy botnets like Mirai to launch massive DDoS attacks.

🔥 **Real-world Example**: The 2016 Mirai botnet attack targeted poorly secured IoT devices, bringing down major parts of the internet. Imagine that—but with power grids.

3. Man-in-the-Middle (MITM) Attacks on Gateway Communications

Gateways are responsible for relaying data between edge devices and central systems. But what happens if an attacker sits in the middle?

Attackers can:

✅ Intercept and alter energy consumption data.

✅ Inject malicious commands to disrupt grid operations.

✅ Steal customer billing information for fraud.

🔥 **Real-world Example**: In 2020, security researchers demonstrated how they could manipulate smart meter data in transit, tricking the system into reporting fake power usage.

4. Exploiting Insecure APIs

Most modern edge devices talk to each other using APIs. But if those APIs aren't secured, it's game over.

Attackers can:

✅ Use API fuzzing to discover unprotected endpoints.

✅ Send malicious API requests to gain unauthorized access.

✅ Leak sensitive grid data via insecure API calls.

🔥 **Real-world Example**: In 2021, an API vulnerability in a major EV charging network exposed customer data, charging logs, and even allowed attackers to disable chargers remotely.

5. Supply Chain Attacks on Edge Firmware & Hardware

Why break into a device when you can just compromise it before it's even installed?

Attackers can:

✅ Inject malicious firmware updates that create backdoors.

✅ Embed hardware Trojans during manufacturing.

✅ Tamper with software dependencies to introduce vulnerabilities.

🔥 **Real-world Example**: The SolarWinds hack (2020) was a massive supply chain attack that compromised thousands of networks worldwide. Now imagine that level of attack—but against power grids.

Defending Against Edge Device & Gateway Attacks
Now that we know the risks, let's talk about how to fight back.

1. Change Default Credentials. Immediately.

Use strong, unique passwords for all devices.

Implement multi-factor authentication (MFA) where possible.

2. Keep Firmware & Software Updated. No Excuses.

Automate regular security patches for edge devices.

Use firmware integrity checks to detect tampering.

3. Encrypt Everything. Seriously.

Use TLS/SSL encryption for all communications.

Implement end-to-end encryption (E2EE) to prevent MITM attacks.

4. Lock Down API Security

Use API authentication tokens to restrict access.

Implement rate limiting to prevent brute-force attacks.

5. Monitor for Anomalies in Real-Time

Deploy intrusion detection systems (IDS) for IoT traffic.

Use AI-driven analytics to flag suspicious activity.

Final Thoughts: Hackers Love the Edge—Let's Not Make It Easy for Them

Smart grids are evolving, and edge computing is making energy distribution smarter, faster, and more efficient. But if we don't secure edge devices and gateways, hackers will turn them into their personal playgrounds.

So, if you're in charge of smart grid security, remember this golden rule: If a device is connected, it's hackable. Protect it like your electricity bill depends on it—because one day, it just might. ⚡🔒

7.3 Malware and Ransomware in Edge-Enabled Smart Grid Systems

Ah, malware and ransomware—the cockroaches of the cyber world. No matter how hard we try, they just keep crawling back, evolving into new, nastier forms. But here's the thing: when these digital pests infest your laptop, you might lose some files and have a bad day. When they hit smart grids and edge devices? We're talking power outages, massive financial losses, and even threats to human safety.

Now, why do hackers love targeting the smart grid? Simple. It's connected, complex, and often outdated—the perfect recipe for cyber mischief. And with edge computing bringing even more devices into the energy ecosystem, the attack surface is bigger than ever. So let's break down how malware and ransomware infiltrate edge-enabled smart grids and, more importantly, how we can fight back.

How Malware and Ransomware Infect Smart Grid Edge Devices

Attackers have an arsenal of tricks to infect edge-enabled systems. Here are the most common entry points:

1. Phishing and Social Engineering (Yep, It Still Works)

Despite all the fancy tech, humans are still the weakest link in cybersecurity. Hackers know this and use phishing emails, fake login pages, and social engineering to trick employees into:

✅ Clicking malicious links that download malware.

✅ Installing fake software updates laced with ransomware.

✅ Giving away login credentials to critical systems.

🔥 **Real-World Example**: In 2021, Colonial Pipeline was hit with ransomware due to a compromised VPN password—causing massive fuel shortages in the U.S. Now imagine that happening to the electric grid.

2. Exploiting Unpatched Vulnerabilities in Edge Devices

Many edge devices—like smart meters, IoT gateways, and energy controllers—run on outdated firmware. Hackers love this because it means they can:

✅ Use remote code execution (RCE) to install malware.

✅ Deploy rootkits that persist even after reboots.

✅ Take full control of the device without anyone noticing.

🔥 **Real-World Example**: The BlackEnergy malware (used in the 2015 Ukraine power grid attack) targeted unpatched industrial control systems (ICS), shutting down power for over 230,000 people.

3. Supply Chain Attacks (The Sneaky Backdoor)

Why hack a system directly when you can infect it before it's even installed? That's the beauty of supply chain attacks. Hackers can:

✅ Compromise firmware updates from trusted vendors.

✅ Inject malware-laced software dependencies into grid systems.

✅ Deploy hardware backdoors in edge computing chips.

🔥 **Real-World Example**: The SolarWinds attack (2020) compromised thousands of government and private networks by injecting malware into trusted software updates.

4. USB & Physical Access Attacks (Because Sometimes Hackers Just Walk In)

If an attacker can physically plug in a malicious USB drive, it's game over. Edge devices often lack strong access controls, making them prime targets for:

✅ USB malware drops (like the infamous Stuxnet attack).

✅ Evil Maid attacks (where a hacker gains short-term physical access).

✅ Keyloggers and remote access trojans (RATs).

🔥 **Real-World Example**: The Stuxnet worm (2010) spread via USB drives to sabotage Iranian nuclear facilities. Imagine a version of Stuxnet tailored for the smart grid.

The Devastating Impact of Ransomware on Smart Grids

So, what happens when ransomware locks up critical smart grid systems? Nothing good. Here's what's at stake:

1. Power Outages & Service Disruptions

Ransomware can encrypt operational technology (OT) systems, shutting down:

🏛 SCADA systems that control power distribution.
🏛 Smart meters, causing billing and outage issues.
🏛 EV charging networks, leaving vehicles stranded.

🔥 **Real-World Example**: In 2022, a ransomware attack on UK-based renewable energy provider Inverter Energy crippled power distribution in multiple regions.

2. Financial & Data Losses

Ransomware doesn't just lock files—it can steal sensitive energy data before encryption. That means:

💰 Huge ransom payments (often in cryptocurrency).
📉 Stock price crashes for utility companies.
🔒 Leaked customer data leading to lawsuits.

🔥 **Real-World Example**: In 2020, Elexon (UK power grid operator) suffered a ransomware attack, disrupting critical energy balancing operations.

3. National Security Threats

If hackers target a nation's smart grid infrastructure, it could:

⚠️ Cause mass blackouts and economic damage.
⚠️ Disrupt military and emergency services.
⚠️ Be exploited by nation-state attackers (Russia, China, North Korea).

🔥 **Real-World Example**: The 2015 Ukraine power grid attack was linked to Russian cyber groups, showing how cyber warfare can cripple a country's energy sector.

How to Defend Against Smart Grid Malware & Ransomware

The good news? We can fight back. Here's how:

1. Implement Zero Trust Security

Assume every device and user is potentially compromised.

Use multi-factor authentication (MFA) for all remote access.

Apply role-based access control (RBAC) to limit permissions.

2. Patch and Update Everything (Yes, Everything)

Regularly update firmware and software for all edge devices.

Monitor and apply security patches for ICS vulnerabilities.

Use automated vulnerability scanners to detect weaknesses.

3. Deploy AI-Driven Threat Detection

Use AI-powered security analytics to spot unusual network activity.

Implement intrusion detection systems (IDS/IPS) for IoT traffic.

Monitor real-time grid anomalies to detect ransomware behavior.

4. Harden API & Network Security

Encrypt all smart grid communications (TLS, VPNs, SSH).

Restrict API access with strong authentication.

Segment networks to prevent malware from spreading laterally.

5. Train Employees & Enforce Cyber Hygiene

Conduct anti-phishing training for grid operators.

Ban USB drives and enforce strict physical security.

Regularly test incident response plans with ransomware simulations.

Final Thoughts: The Smart Grid vs. The Bad Guys

The rise of edge computing makes smart grids faster, smarter, and more efficient—but also more vulnerable to cyber threats. Malware and ransomware aren't going away anytime soon, and hackers are only getting bolder.

So, what's the game plan? Stay paranoid, patch aggressively, and always assume the worst. Because when it comes to smart grid security, it's not a matter of IF an attack will happen—it's a matter of WHEN.

And trust me, you don't want to be the one explaining to your boss why the city's lights just went out. ⚡💀

7.4 Attacking Virtual Power Plants and Distributed Energy Resources (DER)

Alright, let's talk about Virtual Power Plants (VPPs) and Distributed Energy Resources (DER)—because apparently, one giant, centralized power grid wasn't chaotic enough. Instead, we now have thousands of smaller, decentralized power sources, from rooftop solar panels to Tesla Powerwalls, all connected via the Internet. It's like upgrading from a single megastore to a massive online marketplace—except, you know, with life-sustaining electricity at stake.

And if there's one thing we've learned in cybersecurity, it's that the more devices you connect, the more attack surfaces you create. Hackers aren't just interested in messing with your home's smart thermostat anymore—they're looking at ways to manipulate entire regions' energy supply, crash the grid, and maybe even make a few bucks while doing it. So, let's dig into how cybercriminals can attack VPPs and DERs—and how we can stop them before we end up in the dark.

What Are Virtual Power Plants (VPPs) and Distributed Energy Resources (DER)?

Before we go full hacker mode, let's clarify what we're dealing with:

💡 Distributed Energy Resources (DER)

DER refers to small-scale power sources that generate electricity near the point of use rather than at a big, centralized power plant. These include:

Solar panels on rooftops.

Wind turbines in small farms or communities.

Battery storage systems (like Tesla Powerwalls).

Electric vehicles (EVs) feeding power back to the grid.

⚡ Virtual Power Plants (VPPs)

A VPP is like the Uber of energy—instead of one big plant generating power, it aggregates multiple DERs, managing them like a single entity. VPPs:

Use software and IoT devices to control distributed resources.

Balance power demand and supply in real time.

Sell excess electricity back to the main grid or to consumers.

Sounds great, right? Until a hacker decides to take control and turn our smart, decentralized energy system into a chaotic, electrified nightmare.

How Hackers Can Attack VPPs and DERs

1. Hijacking IoT-Controlled Power Systems

Since VPPs rely on IoT sensors, smart inverters, and cloud-based platforms, hackers can:

◆ Manipulate power generation—shutting down solar panels or battery storage.
◆ Trigger grid instability by turning multiple DERs on/off at once.
◆ Cause voltage fluctuations that damage electrical infrastructure.

🔥 **Real-World Example**: In 2021, security researchers demonstrated how insecure IoT-enabled solar inverters could be remotely controlled, posing a serious risk to energy grids.

2. Exploiting Communication Protocol Vulnerabilities

DERs and VPPs rely on protocols like DNP3, Modbus, IEC 61850, and MQTT. If these aren't properly secured, attackers can:

🏛 Intercept and alter energy commands.
🏛 Inject malicious firmware into smart energy controllers.
🏛 Conduct Man-in-the-Middle (MITM) attacks to disrupt grid coordination.

🔥 **Real-World Example**: The Industroyer malware (linked to Russia) exploited ICS protocols to disrupt Ukraine's power grid. Similar tactics could be used on DERs.

3. Ransomware Attacks on VPP Control Systems

Since VPPs are software-driven, attackers can:

💰 Encrypt control systems and demand ransom.
💰 Lock out operators from managing DERs.
💰 Disrupt grid balancing, forcing energy providers into a crisis.

🔥 **Real-World Example**: In 2020, the EKANS ransomware specifically targeted ICS and energy grid components, proving ransomware is no longer just an IT problem—it's now a power problem too.

4. Manipulating Energy Markets & Fraud

By hacking VPP systems, cybercriminals can:

📈 Artificially inflate energy prices by reducing supply.

📉 Sell stolen energy credits on the black market.

☐ Commit billing fraud by altering DER production reports.

🔥 **Real-World Example**: The infamous Energetic Bear hacking group has been linked to cyber-espionage targeting energy companies, likely aiming to disrupt energy markets.

The Devastating Impact of VPP & DER Cyberattacks

So, what happens if hackers take control of VPPs and DERs? Spoiler: It's bad.

⚠️ 1. Regional Blackouts & Grid Instability

If enough DERs go offline simultaneously, parts of the grid could collapse.

Voltage spikes could fry electrical equipment and lead to widespread outages.

Renewable energy supply chains could be disrupted.

🔥 **Example**: The 2003 Northeast blackout (which wasn't cyber-related) showed how small failures can snowball into massive power outages. Now imagine that, but hacked.

⚠️ 2. Economic Losses & Energy Market Manipulation

Ransomware or fraud in VPP systems could cost millions in damages.

Power shortages could skyrocket electricity prices.

Energy theft and manipulation could disrupt entire economies.

🔥 **Example**: In 2021, hackers attempted to poison a Florida water plant using ICS vulnerabilities—proving that critical infrastructure is a prime target.

⚠️ 3. National Security Risks

Nation-state actors could use DER attacks as cyberwarfare.

Military bases and emergency services could lose power.

Hackers could cripple smart cities relying on VPP-driven grids.

🔥 **Example**: U.S. officials have warned that China and Russia are actively probing energy infrastructure for cyber vulnerabilities.

How to Defend VPPs and DERs from Cyberattacks

🔒 **1. Secure IoT Devices & Communication Protocols**

✅ Use end-to-end encryption (TLS, VPNs, SSH) for DER data.

✅ Apply secure authentication (MFA, certificates) for device access.

✅ Regularly patch firmware and software on smart inverters and controllers.

🔲 **2. Implement Network Segmentation & Zero Trust Security**

✅ Isolate DER control networks from public-facing internet access.

✅ Use firewalls and IDS/IPS to detect anomalous energy traffic.

✅ Enforce Zero Trust principles—assume no device is automatically trusted.

⚠️ **3. Deploy AI-Driven Threat Detection & Incident Response**

✅ Use AI-powered analytics to detect abnormal DER behavior.

✅ Implement real-time monitoring for VPP energy fluctuations.

✅ Have automated shutdown protocols in case of cyberattacks.

Final Thoughts: The Cyber Arms Race for the Smart Grid

Virtual Power Plants and Distributed Energy Resources are the future of energy, offering cleaner, more efficient power generation. But with that decentralization comes new security risks. Hackers aren't just interested in stealing data anymore—they're manipulating power grids, influencing energy markets, and waging cyberwarfare.

So, if you're working in energy cybersecurity, your job just got a whole lot harder. But hey—at least it's never boring, right? Stay paranoid, stay patched, and don't let the bad guys pull the plug. ⚡💀

7.5 Securing Grid Edge Computing Against Emerging Threats

You know, securing Grid Edge Computing sometimes feels like trying to baby-proof a house while an army of toddlers (aka hackers) actively looks for sharp objects, electrical sockets, and anything else they can break. The smart grid is evolving, shifting computing power closer to the edge—which means faster data processing, real-time analytics, and reduced latency. Sounds great, right? But it also means more attack surfaces, more vulnerabilities, and more sleepless nights for cybersecurity pros.

Hackers aren't just targeting big data centers anymore—they're going after the edge where small, distributed computing nodes handle critical grid operations. And if they succeed? Well, imagine entire regions losing power, manipulated energy prices, or even controlled blackouts. So, let's dive into how we can secure Grid Edge Computing before cybercriminals turn our power infrastructure into their personal playground.

What Is Grid Edge Computing, and Why Should We Care?

Grid Edge Computing refers to processing data closer to where it's generated—like at smart meters, IoT sensors, DERs (Distributed Energy Resources), and EV charging stations. Instead of sending every bit of data to a central cloud or control center, edge devices make real-time decisions locally to improve efficiency and reduce network load.

💡 Why It's Awesome:

Faster response times for demand fluctuations.

Better reliability for renewable energy sources.

Lower bandwidth consumption by processing data locally.

⚠️ Why It's a Security Nightmare:

More distributed attack points (thousands of smart devices instead of one central server).

Increased risk of device takeovers and data manipulation.

Harder to monitor edge devices in real time due to their remote locations.

And since Grid Edge Computing is deeply tied to IoT, we get all the fun IoT security problems too—weak authentication, outdated firmware, and unsecured communication channels.

Emerging Threats to Grid Edge Computing

1. Edge Device Hijacking & Botnets

Smart inverters, meters, and controllers aren't just managing power—they're potential zombie soldiers in massive botnets. A compromised fleet of edge devices can:

⬜⬜ Launch DDoS attacks on grid control centers.
🖫 Spread malware across the smart grid.
☻ Manipulate local power distribution to destabilize regions.

🔥 **Example**: The Mirai botnet infected millions of IoT devices, turning them into attack weapons. Now imagine that but with smart grid devices—scary, right?

2. Man-in-the-Middle (MITM) Attacks on Edge Communications

Edge devices talk to control centers, cloud servers, and each other. But if attackers can intercept those communications?

📡 They can alter grid control commands.
ⓘ Manipulate energy pricing and metering data.
⚕ Trigger false shutdowns or overloading events.

🔥 **Example**: Industroyer 2, linked to Russian hackers, targeted energy grid communications, proving that MITM attacks on power infrastructure aren't hypothetical—they're happening.

3. Ransomware and Malware at the Edge

Since edge devices are often less secure, they're prime targets for malware and ransomware. Attackers can:

🔐 Encrypt control systems and demand ransom.

⚡ Take edge nodes offline, disrupting power stability.

💰 Threaten to sell stolen energy data on the dark web.

🔥 **Example**: EKANS ransomware specifically targeted industrial control systems, showing that energy infrastructure is now a favorite ransomware target.

4. Supply Chain Attacks on Edge Hardware & Software

Grid edge devices rely on third-party hardware, firmware, and software updates. If attackers compromise the supply chain, they can:

⚠️ Embed malware in firmware updates.

⚠️ Introduce backdoors at the manufacturer level.

⚠️ Disrupt the entire grid by pushing malicious patches.

🔥 **Example**: The SolarWinds attack showed how supply chain vulnerabilities can compromise thousands of critical systems at once.

How to Secure Grid Edge Computing Against Cyber Threats

🔒 1. Secure the Devices from the Start

Zero Trust should be the default for every edge device. Assume that no device is safe until it's fully verified.

✓ Use secure boot mechanisms to prevent tampered firmware from running.

✓ Enforce strong authentication (multi-factor authentication, certificates).

✓ Regularly patch and update firmware—no more "set it and forget it."

🔐 2. Encrypt & Authenticate All Communications

Since MITM attacks are a major threat, encryption is non-negotiable.

✓ Use TLS, VPNs, and SSH for all grid-edge communications.

✓ Implement device certificates to prevent unauthorized connections.

✓ Deploy network anomaly detection to catch suspicious activity early.

⚠️ 3. Segment the Network (No More Open Access)

Grid operators need to limit access between systems.

✅ Separate edge devices from critical control systems using firewalls.

✅ Deploy micro-segmentation so that compromised devices can't spread malware.

✅ Use role-based access controls to restrict who (or what) can send grid commands.

☐ 4. AI-Driven Threat Detection & Automated Response

Cyberattacks on grid edge computing happen too fast for manual response. AI can help.

✅ Use AI-driven anomaly detection to spot unusual energy fluctuations.

✅ Automate security patching for edge devices.

✅ Deploy self-healing security—if an attack is detected, the device should auto-quarantine.

🏭 5. Secure the Supply Chain

Grid edge security isn't just about software—it starts with trustworthy hardware and vendors.

✅ Vet third-party vendors and require security audits.

✅ Use hardware-based security (TPMs, HSMs) to prevent tampering.

✅ Check for backdoors in firmware updates before deployment.

The Future of Grid Edge Security: Challenges & Innovations

The shift to decentralized energy is unstoppable—but so is the cybersecurity arms race. New AI-powered defenses, blockchain for securing energy transactions, and quantum encryption are all emerging solutions to protect the grid. But here's the thing:

Attackers aren't waiting. They're already probing smart meters, inverters, and grid controllers for weaknesses.

Defenders need to move faster. The old IT security model doesn't work when you're dealing with real-time power grids.

Automation is the only way forward. If we don't let AI-powered security handle some of the load, hackers will outpace us.

The grid edge is where the future of energy happens—but it's also where the biggest cyber battles will be fought. So, as we keep pushing toward a smarter, decentralized power grid, let's make sure we're not just making it smart, but also secure.

And if we get it wrong? Well, let's just say you don't want to be the guy explaining a nationwide blackout because of a hacked smart toaster. ⚡😄

Chapter 8: Hacking Electric Vehicle (EV) Charging Infrastructure

Picture this: You've just bought your shiny new electric vehicle (EV), ready to zip around the city with zero emissions and all the perks. You pull into the nearest charging station, plug in, and relax, knowing you're doing your part for the environment. But, what if your EV's charging station isn't as secure as it seems? What if, instead of charging your car, it's charging up a hacker's tools? Enter the world of EV charging infrastructure—where convenience meets vulnerability. Whether it's hijacking payment systems, tampering with charging processes, or even draining a whole fleet of EVs, this chapter dives into how those very stations designed to fuel your eco-friendly ride could become the next cyber battlefield. Spoiler alert: Hackers don't just target the car; they go after the whole charging network. Let's plug into the risks and vulnerabilities of this electrifying technology!

In this chapter, we examine the cybersecurity risks associated with Electric Vehicle (EV) charging infrastructure, which has become an essential component of the rapidly expanding EV ecosystem. As the number of electric vehicles on the road grows, so does the need for secure, efficient charging stations. These charging stations, often interconnected through cloud-based networks, are vulnerable to various cyber threats, including data breaches, system manipulation, and denial-of-service (DoS) attacks. We will explore the key vulnerabilities in EV charging networks, the potential consequences of an attack, and the methods used by hackers to exploit these weaknesses. Additionally, we will provide insight into best practices and security measures that can be implemented to safeguard the integrity of EV charging infrastructure, ensuring both user safety and system resilience in the face of growing cyber threats.

8.1 Overview of EV Charging Networks and Protocols (OCPP, ISO 15118)

You ever plug in your phone at a public charging station and wonder, "Could this thing be stealing my data?" Well, imagine that concern—but at a much bigger scale, with electric vehicles (EVs), smart chargers, and an entire power grid in the mix.

EV charging networks are growing at lightning speed (pun intended). We're moving from a few scattered charging stations to a massive, interconnected web of smart chargers that talk to cars, power grids, and even payment systems. But with all that convenience comes a huge attack surface—because every time an EV "handshakes" with a charger, there's a chance a hacker is waiting to high-five it right into chaos.

Before we get into hacking EV charging infrastructure, let's break down how this whole ecosystem works, and why protocols like OCPP and ISO 15118 are both essential and potentially dangerous if not properly secured.

The EV Charging Ecosystem: Who Talks to Who?

EV charging isn't just "plugging in and powering up." It involves multiple players communicating over networks that can be hijacked if not secured. Let's meet the cast:

EVs (Electric Vehicles) – The main customer, looking for a charge.

Charging Stations (EVSEs - Electric Vehicle Supply Equipment) – The "fuel pumps" of the electric world.

Charging Network Operators (CNOs) – Manage fleets of charging stations and handle payments.

Utilities and Grid Operators – Control electricity distribution and pricing.

Back-End Cloud Services – Store charging data, user credentials, and transactions.

All these players talk to each other using communication protocols, which is where OCPP and ISO 15118 come in.

OCPP (Open Charge Point Protocol): The Language of Charging Stations

Think of OCPP as the Wi-Fi of EV charging—it's an open standard that lets charging stations talk to the cloud, ensuring interoperability across different manufacturers.

⚡ Why It's Popular:

✅ Open-source & widely adopted – No vendor lock-in.

✅ Supports remote management – CNOs can update, troubleshoot, and monitor chargers.

✅ Handles payments & authorization – Users can pay with apps, RFID cards, or subscriptions.

⚠️ Why It's a Security Risk:

🚨 Many stations still use OCPP 1.5 & 1.6, which lack proper encryption.
🚨 Man-in-the-Middle (MITM) attacks can intercept charging commands.
🚨 Weak authentication can let attackers spoof commands (e.g., stopping someone's charge remotely).

🔥 Real-World Attack Example:

Hackers once manipulated public charging stations using OCPP flaws, remotely shutting them down and altering pricing models. Imagine charging fees spiking to $100 per kWh overnight—yikes.

The solution? OCPP 2.0.1, which finally introduced stronger security features like TLS encryption and certificate-based authentication. But guess what? Most charging stations still haven't upgraded.

ISO 15118: The "Plug & Charge" Revolution

ISO 15118 is the standard that makes Plug & Charge (PnC) possible—just plug in your car, and it automatically authenticates and starts charging without the need for apps, cards, or QR codes. No more fumbling with payment methods.

💡 Why It's Cool:

✅ **Seamless user experience** – No need for apps or RFID cards.
✅ **Automated authentication** – The car and charger exchange digital certificates for a secure handshake.
✅ **Bidirectional charging (V2G - Vehicle-to-Grid)** – Your car can send power back to the grid during peak demand.

⚠️ Why It's a Hacker's Playground:

🚨 **Digital certificates can be stolen or forged** – Attackers can charge for free or impersonate other vehicles.

⚨ **Man-in-the-Middle attacks** – If encryption isn't properly implemented, hackers can intercept Plug & Charge sessions.

⚨ **Vehicle-to-Grid (V2G) exploits** – If an EV charger is compromised, it could disrupt grid stability by injecting fake power fluctuations.

🔥 **Real-World Risk:**

Researchers have shown how bad actors could steal charging credentials from an ISO 15118-enabled system, effectively letting them charge for free at someone else's expense. Worse? Attackers could spoof entire fleets of EVs, draining local power grids.

How Hackers Target EV Charging Networks

1️⃣ **Fake Charging Stations** – Attackers set up rogue charging points that steal authentication credentials.

2️⃣ **MITM Attacks on OCPP & ISO 15118** – Hackers intercept commands, modify power delivery, or shut down stations remotely.

3️⃣ **Ransomware on Charging Networks** – Entire fleets of chargers are locked down until ransom is paid.

4️⃣ **V2G Manipulation** – Attackers inject power surges into the grid, causing blackouts or price manipulations.

Securing EV Charging Networks

So, how do we stop cybercriminals from turning EV chargers into digital ATMs and attack vectors?

🔒 **1. Upgrade to OCPP 2.0.1 & Enforce Strong Encryption**

Mandate TLS 1.2 or higher to prevent eavesdropping.

Require strong authentication (certificates, tokens) for all network connections.

Monitor network traffic for unusual activity.

🔐 **2. Secure ISO 15118 Plug & Charge Implementations**

Use hardware security modules (HSMs) to protect digital certificates.

Implement certificate revocation lists (CRLs) to invalidate stolen credentials.

Enable two-way authentication between vehicles and chargers.

⚠️ 3. Defend Against Physical Tampering

Harden charging stations with tamper-proof enclosures.

Implement intrusion detection for unauthorized access.

Use geofencing to track and disable rogue chargers.

☐ 4. AI-Driven Threat Detection & Automated Response

Detect unusual charging patterns (e.g., mass unauthorized free charging).

Auto-quarantine compromised chargers from the network.

Use blockchain for transaction integrity in payment systems.

Final Thoughts: EV Charging Security Is a Work in Progress

EV charging networks are still evolving, and so are the threats against them. While OCPP 2.0.1 and ISO 15118 improve security, adoption is slow, and legacy vulnerabilities remain a massive problem.

But let's be real—EVs aren't going anywhere. The future is electric, and we need to secure charging networks before hackers figure out how to drain our batteries—both literally and financially.

And if we don't? Well… enjoy paying for someone else's Tesla charge while wondering why your own EV mysteriously refuses to charge past 10%. 🔌⚡😂

8.2 Exploiting Vulnerabilities in Smart Charging Stations

Ah, smart charging stations—the gas stations of the future, except now they come with Wi-Fi, cloud connectivity, and more potential attack surfaces than a Swiss cheese firewall.

These aren't just dumb power outlets; they're full-fledged IoT devices loaded with communication protocols, payment processing, and remote access capabilities. And you know what that means? Hackers are practically salivating.

Imagine this: You pull up to a public charging station, plug in your EV, grab a coffee, and come back to find your charging session mysteriously stopped. You try again. Nothing. Then, you get a notification—"Your charging account has been drained. Have a nice day!" Congratulations, you've just been hacked!

This chapter dives into how attackers exploit smart charging stations, exposing flaws in authentication, firmware, communication protocols, and even physical security. Let's break it down before your next charge turns into a cyber nightmare.

How Smart Charging Stations Work

A smart charging station (also known as EVSE - Electric Vehicle Supply Equipment) is more than just a plug. It's a mini-computer that:

Authenticates Users – Verifies drivers through RFID cards, mobile apps, or Plug & Charge (ISO 15118).

Communicates with the Grid – Talks to the power provider to adjust load and pricing dynamically.

Handles Payments – Securely (or not) processes transactions via credit cards, mobile apps, or cloud accounts.

Receives Remote Updates – Can be patched, restarted, or even disabled remotely by charging network operators.

Now, let's look at where the vulnerabilities hide.

1. Authentication and Payment Exploits

💳 RFID & Mobile App Attacks

Most public chargers authenticate users via RFID cards or mobile apps. But these systems are often:

🔒 **Poorly encrypted** → Attackers can clone RFID cards or intercept app credentials.

💀 **Vulnerable to replay attacks** → If the authentication isn't using session tokens, a hacker can simply replay a valid session to steal a charge.

🔥 **Real-World Example**: A hacker in Europe cloned an RFID card used for EV charging and sold unlimited charging sessions on the dark web. Customers thought they were getting free electricity—until their real accounts got drained.

💰 **Payment System Weaknesses**

If the backend payment system is misconfigured, attackers can:

Bypass authentication and charge for free.

Modify charge rates to overbill unsuspecting users.

Steal credit card data if proper encryption isn't enforced.

💀 **Fun Fact**: Some older charging stations still use hardcoded default admin passwords, like admin123. A little Shodan search, and boom—free charging for life.

2. Remote Exploits & Network Attacks

Since smart chargers are connected to the internet, they can be hacked remotely. Let's look at how.

🔌 **Open Charge Point Protocol (OCPP) Exploits**

OCPP is the most common communication standard used by EV charging stations. But... older versions (1.5 & 1.6) lack encryption, making them a prime target for:

💀 **Man-in-the-Middle (MITM) attacks** – Hackers can intercept commands, modify charging rates, or even disable stations remotely.
💀 **Session hijacking** – Attackers can steal user credentials and start unauthorized charging sessions.

💀 **Scary Scenario**: Researchers found unpatched OCPP vulnerabilities that allowed attackers to:

Stop any charging session remotely

Turn a network of chargers into a botnet for DDoS attacks

Inject malware into backend cloud systems

⚖ **What's Worse**? Many charging stations don't enforce firmware updates, meaning once a vulnerability is discovered, it stays vulnerable for years.

3. Physical Attacks: The Hands-On Hacker's Delight

Not all hackers work from behind a screen. Some like to get their hands dirty.

🔌 USB & Debug Ports

Some charging stations still have open USB or debug ports hidden inside their casings. Attackers can:

Plug in malicious devices to extract firmware & encryption keys.

Exploit bootloader vulnerabilities to install backdoored firmware.

Tamper with relay switches to disrupt charging operations.

🔥 **Real-World Attack**: A hacker at a security conference demonstrated how a hidden USB port on a public charger allowed him to gain root access, reprogram the station, and enable free charging permanently.

🔧 Physical Tampering

Some older charging stations lack tamper detection. Attackers can:

Cut power lines to disrupt services.

Replace payment terminals with skimmers to steal credit card data.

Modify voltage outputs to damage EVs plugged into the charger.

☠ **Nightmare Fuel**: Imagine plugging in your Tesla, only to have a maliciously modified charger send a voltage spike that fries your battery. That's a six-figure hack right there.

4. Wireless & Bluetooth Attacks

Some smart chargers use Bluetooth or Wi-Fi for mobile app control. But…

🔒 **Default Wi-Fi credentials** – Some charging stations still ship with hardcoded "admin/admin" logins.

🔒 **Bluetooth pairing flaws** – Attackers can spoof connections and take over charger controls.

🔒 **Wi-Fi sniffing attacks** – If a charger connects to an open network, hackers can eavesdrop on OCPP commands.

🔥 **Fun Attack**: Security researchers were able to remotely start and stop charging sessions by brute-forcing Bluetooth connections on certain public chargers.

How to Defend Against These Attacks

Smart charging stations need better security—here's how operators and users can protect them.

🔒 1. Secure Authentication

✓ RFID encryption → Prevent cloning attacks.

✓ Multi-factor authentication (MFA) → Reduce credential theft risks.

✓ Session tokenization → Prevent replay attacks.

🔲 2. Secure OCPP & Network Communications

✓ Upgrade to OCPP 2.0.1 → Enforce encryption (TLS 1.2+).

✓ Segment charging stations on separate VLANs to isolate attacks.

✓ Monitor for unusual traffic (DDoS, command injection attempts).

💀 3. Harden Physical Security

✓ Remove unnecessary USB/debug ports.

✅ Install tamper-detection sensors.

✅ Encrypt firmware updates to prevent rogue modifications.

📡 4. Secure Wireless & Bluetooth Access

✅ Disable unused wireless interfaces.

✅ Require strong authentication for remote access.

✅ Monitor for rogue Bluetooth/Wi-Fi connections.

Final Thoughts: If It's Smart, It's Hackable

Smart charging stations make life easier, but they're also an attack vector waiting to happen. Whether it's stealing charging sessions, hijacking OCPP connections, or tampering with power outputs, hackers have plenty of ways to exploit poorly secured EVSEs.

The good news? Security is improving—but many existing stations remain vulnerable. Until every operator enforces strong authentication, encrypts communications, and patches firmware, hackers will keep finding ways to juice up their EVs for free—on your dime.

So next time you plug in… double-check that charging station. It might just be charging more than your car—it could be charging straight into a hacker's hands. 🔌 💀

8.3 Attacking Vehicle-to-Grid (V2G) Communications

Ah, Vehicle-to-Grid (V2G)—the ultimate dream of a futuristic, energy-efficient world where your EV isn't just a car but also a mini power plant. Imagine your Tesla not only taking electricity from the grid but also selling it back when you're not using it. It's like turning your car into a side hustle—except, as with any "smart" system, hackers are also eyeing it like a buffet of vulnerabilities.

Now, what happens if an attacker manipulates the system? Suddenly, instead of selling power to the grid, your EV starts draining your home's electricity, or worse, it's remotely commanded to discharge its entire battery while you're sleeping. That's not just an inconvenience—it's an open door to cyber warfare on energy infrastructure. So, let's dive into how hackers can exploit V2G communications and what can be done to stop them.

What is Vehicle-to-Grid (V2G)?

V2G is a two-way energy exchange system where EVs can:

🔌 Charge from the grid when electricity demand is low.
⚡ Discharge energy back to the grid during peak demand.
💰 Optimize energy costs by buying cheap and selling high.

To enable this, V2G relies on a complex web of communication protocols, cloud-based energy markets, and automated commands between EVs, charging stations, and the grid.

And where there's communication, there's exploitation potential.

1. Man-in-the-Middle (MITM) Attacks on V2G Communications

☠️ **How It Works**

Most V2G transactions are sent over the internet using protocols like OCPP, ISO 15118, and MQTT. If these communications aren't properly encrypted, an attacker can:

Intercept energy commands.

Modify charge/discharge instructions.

Impersonate a charging station to trick the EV.

Imagine a hacker setting up a rogue charging station that falsely tells cars, "Hey, the grid needs your power—discharge now!" But in reality? That energy is getting drained into the attacker's private energy storage system.

💡 **Real-world concern**: Security researchers have already demonstrated how weak encryption in OCPP (Open Charge Point Protocol) can allow MITM attacks, where commands are modified in transit—and the same risks apply to V2G.

2. EV Hijacking via Fake Firmware Updates

🔧 **How It Works**

Most EVs receive over-the-air (OTA) firmware updates to improve performance and security. But what happens if an attacker injects malicious firmware into the update process?

🔊 **A compromised update could:**

Modify how the vehicle responds to V2G commands (e.g., always discharge when connected).

Cause permanent battery damage by manipulating charge cycles.

Give attackers remote control over an entire fleet of EVs.

💀 **Worst-case scenario**? A hacker compromises multiple EV fleets and commands them all to discharge power simultaneously, destabilizing the grid.

🔥 **Historical Reference**: The infamous Mirai botnet turned IoT devices into an army of zombie machines. What if a fleet of EVs became a Mirai-style energy weapon?

3. Unauthorized Energy Theft & Billing Fraud

☐ **How It Works**

Many V2G transactions involve automated billing, where the EV owner gets paid for feeding electricity back to the grid. But if that payment system isn't secure... well, let's just say hackers love free money.

🔊 **Attackers can:**

Fake energy transactions to claim payments for electricity they never supplied.

Exploit billing rate fluctuations to get paid more than they should.

Redirect payments meant for one EV owner to another account.

💡 **Fun Hack**: An attacker could program a fleet of compromised EVs to "sell" electricity to the grid but never actually discharge—stealing cash without losing a single watt.

4. Grid Destabilization Attacks

✸ The Nightmare Scenario

One of the biggest concerns in V2G security isn't just individual attacks—it's how a large-scale attack could take down an entire energy grid.

Imagine this:

A hacker compromises a large number of EVs.

They command them all to discharge simultaneously, flooding the grid with excess electricity.

Seconds later, they command them to stop discharging and start charging at full capacity.

This massive demand spike causes a grid-wide blackout.

📟 This isn't just theory. Researchers have shown that coordinated EV discharging could create grid instabilities that could take entire power networks offline.

💡 **Scary Real-World Example**: Attackers in Ukraine used malware (Industroyer) to cause power outages in 2016. A V2G-powered attack could be even more devastating because EVs are spread across an entire country.

5. Exploiting Weak Authentication in ISO 15118 (Plug & Charge)

🔌 How It Works

The ISO 15118 standard allows EVs to authenticate automatically when plugged in—no need for RFID cards or mobile apps.

📟 The Problem?

Some early implementations don't encrypt authentication tokens.

Attackers could spoof a vehicle's identity and charge on someone else's account.

If the charger doesn't verify the EV's digital certificate, hackers could masquerade as an authorized vehicle and steal energy.

💀 Imagine pulling up to a charging station and realizing someone else has been draining your energy credits remotely.

Defensive Strategies: Securing V2G Communications

To keep V2G safe, stronger security measures need to be implemented across the board.

🔒 **1. Strong Encryption for V2G Protocols**

✅ Use TLS 1.3 for OCPP and ISO 15118 to prevent MITM attacks.

✅ Enforce mutual authentication between EVs, chargers, and grid operators.

▢▢ **2. Secure Firmware Updates**

✅ Digitally sign OTA updates to prevent rogue firmware injections.

✅ Implement rollback protections to detect tampering.

💰 **3. Secure Billing & Energy Transactions**

✅ Use blockchain-based smart contracts to ensure transaction integrity.

✅ Regularly audit billing systems for fraudulent transactions.

⚠▢ **4. Implement Grid Anomaly Detection**

✅ AI-based monitoring can detect suspicious energy patterns.

✅ Rate-limiting discharge commands can prevent mass-discharge attacks.

Final Thoughts: The EV Grid Can Be Hacked—But It Doesn't Have to Be

V2G is an amazing technology—but without strong cybersecurity, it's also a potential disaster waiting to happen. From MITM attacks to energy fraud to grid-wide chaos, attackers have plenty of ways to exploit insecure V2G implementations.

But hey, that doesn't mean we should go back to gas-guzzling cars. It just means the EV industry needs to take security as seriously as they take battery range.

So, next time you plug in your EV, just remember: Your car isn't just charging—it's also a cyber battlefield. Stay secure, stay charged, and don't let hackers ride for free. 🔌💀⚡

8.4 MITM Attacks and Data Exfiltration in EV Infrastructure

Ah, electric vehicles (EVs)—the shiny, high-tech chariots of the future. They whisper silently down the road, save the planet (sort of), and, unfortunately, scream "hack me!" to cybercriminals. EVs aren't just cars anymore; they're rolling IoT devices that sip data just as much as they do electricity. And where there's data, there's a hacker lurking in the shadows, waiting to snoop, steal, and manipulate it.

One of the most dangerous ways attackers can mess with EV infrastructure? Man-in-the-Middle (MITM) attacks. With the right setup, a hacker can sit between an EV and a charging station, quietly intercepting sensitive data, altering commands, or even stealing your payment details while you're just trying to juice up your ride. So buckle up, because we're diving into how MITM attacks work in EV infrastructure, how hackers exfiltrate critical data, and—most importantly—how to keep your car from becoming an all-you-can-eat buffet for cybercriminals.

What's a MITM Attack? And Why Should EV Owners Care?

In simple terms, a Man-in-the-Middle (MITM) attack happens when an attacker intercepts communications between two parties (in this case, an EV and a charging station or backend server) without them realizing it. Think of it as someone secretly listening in on your phone call—except they can also change what's being said.

In the context of EV charging infrastructure, a MITM attack allows hackers to:

Steal authentication credentials and payment data (because let's be real, no one likes paying for electricity when they can make someone else do it).

Manipulate energy transactions, making an EV charge or discharge unpredictably.

Push malicious firmware updates to take control of the vehicle's systems.

Monitor driver behaviors, logging when and where they charge their car—perfect for stalking, tracking, or corporate espionage.

Now, let's look at where the vulnerabilities are and how attackers actually pull this off.

1. Targeting Weak Encryption in Charging Protocols

The Open Charge Point Protocol (OCPP) and ISO 15118 (the so-called "Plug & Charge" standard) are two of the most widely used communication protocols in EV infrastructure. They handle everything from authentication to billing and energy flow management.

💀 The Problem?

Some older versions of these protocols lack proper encryption or use weak cryptographic standards, making them easy to intercept.

🔍 How Hackers Exploit It:

They set up a rogue Wi-Fi access point near a charging station.

When an EV connects to the station over an unsecured network, the hacker intercepts the data exchange.

If weak encryption is used (or none at all), they steal authentication tokens and payment details.

💀 **Worst-case scenario**? The hacker clones the authentication token and starts charging their own EV on your account. Congratulations, you just bought a cybercriminal a free full tank of electrons.

2. Rogue Charging Stations & Evil Twin Attacks

This one's straight-up cyber trickery at its finest. Attackers set up fake charging stations (or hijack real ones) to intercept and alter data exchanges.

💀 How It Works:

A hacker installs a compromised EV charger in a public charging area.

When an EV driver plugs in, the station records their authentication credentials and sends them to the attacker's server.

The hacker can then sell these credentials on the dark web, steal payment info, or impersonate the EV owner on legitimate networks.

💡 **Real-world twist**? Security researchers have already demonstrated that some EV chargers use hardcoded credentials—making them ridiculously easy to hijack.

3. Exploiting Cellular & Wi-Fi Weaknesses in EV Communication

Many modern EVs and charging stations communicate over cellular networks (4G, 5G) or Wi-Fi, allowing them to:

✅ Authenticate with backend servers.

✅ Sync software updates.

✅ Process billing transactions.

🔎 **The Weak Spots:**

Unsecured public Wi-Fi at charging stations.

Weak 4G encryption that allows IMSI catchers (fake cell towers) to intercept data.

Open MQTT brokers that expose real-time charging transactions.

🔍 **How Hackers Exploit It:**

The attacker sets up a fake Wi-Fi hotspot near a charging station, naming it something convincing like "Tesla Supercharger Free Wi-Fi".

EV owners connect unknowingly, allowing the attacker to sniff all unencrypted data passing through.

The hacker extracts session tokens, login credentials, and payment details, using them to spoof an account or commit fraud.

☠ **Worst-case scenario**? If the attacker injects malicious payloads, they could remotely disable an entire fleet of EVs.

4. Data Exfiltration Through Compromised Charging Networks

EV charging stations collect an enormous amount of personal data, including:

🔎 Location history (where you charge your car).
💳 Payment details and transaction logs.
💳 Battery health and charging patterns.
🆔 Vehicle identification numbers (VINs).

If a hacker gains access to a charging network, they can:

Extract location data to track a person's movements.

Steal payment credentials for fraudulent transactions.

Sell driver behavior analytics to third parties.

🔥 **Example Attack**: In 2021, security researchers found that some public EV charging networks were leaking location data of EV owners due to poor API security. Imagine an attacker pinpointing your daily charging habits and using that info for theft, stalking, or even corporate espionage.

How to Defend Against MITM Attacks in EV Infrastructure

🔐 **1. Enforce End-to-End Encryption**

✓ Use TLS 1.3 with strong cipher suites for all OCPP and ISO 15118 communications.

✓ Implement mutual authentication between EVs and charging stations.

☐ **2. Secure EV Firmware & Charging Networks**

✓ Sign firmware updates cryptographically to prevent rogue updates.

✓ Deploy AI-based anomaly detection for real-time threat monitoring.

🚫 **3. Avoid Public Wi-Fi & Untrusted Networks**

✓ Use VPN encryption when connecting to charging networks over Wi-Fi.

✓ Disable automatic Wi-Fi connections to prevent rogue access points from hijacking sessions.

🔍 4. Monitor for Rogue Charging Stations

✓ Verify a charger's legitimacy before plugging in.

✓ Look out for fake SSIDs or unfamiliar Wi-Fi prompts at charging locations.

🔏 5. Demand Stronger Regulations & Security Standards

✓ EV manufacturers and charging providers need to enforce stronger cybersecurity policies before deploying half-baked, insecure tech into the wild.

Final Thoughts: Keep Your EV's Data Locked Tight

The future of EVs and smart charging is exciting, but let's be honest—we're plugging cars into the internet, and that's just asking for trouble. Cybercriminals are already sniffing around, looking for ways to exploit weak encryption, intercept data, and manipulate V2G transactions.

But hey, it's not all doom and gloom. With the right security measures, we can keep our EVs secure, our payment details private, and our charging networks free from MITM attacks and data leaks. So the next time you plug in your car, make sure it's the battery that's getting drained, not your cybersecurity defenses. 🔌⚡🚗💀

8.5 Strengthening Security in EV Charging and V2G Networks

Ah, electric vehicles (EVs). The sleek, futuristic rides that promise a greener planet, lower fuel costs, and—unfortunately—a whole new playground for hackers. As we move towards smarter energy grids and vehicle-to-grid (V2G) integration, security threats are revving up at full speed.

Because let's be real—when you plug your car into a network that also talks to power plants, payment systems, and cloud services, there are bound to be vulnerabilities. Hackers love complex, interconnected systems because one weak link is all it takes to start stealing energy, messing with payments, or even shutting down charging stations. So, how do we keep EV charging networks and V2G communications safe from cyberattacks? Buckle up, because we're about to break it down.

Why Securing EV Charging and V2G Networks Matters

With EV adoption skyrocketing, charging infrastructure is expanding rapidly. These networks are connected to:

Smart grids that manage electricity distribution.

Cloud-based platforms that handle billing and authentication.

Vehicle-to-grid (V2G) systems that let cars send energy back to the grid.

🚨 The Problem?

Weak encryption & authentication leave EV chargers exposed.

Hacked charging stations can steal payment data or inject malware.

Compromised V2G networks can cause power grid instability.

Cybercriminals are already testing these waters. Researchers have found dozens of security flaws in EV chargers, from hardcoded credentials to unencrypted communication channels. If we don't tighten security, EV infrastructure could become a prime target for large-scale cyberattacks.

1. Securing EV Charging Stations from Cyber Threats

EV chargers aren't just power outlets—they're IoT devices with embedded systems, wireless connectivity, and software that's often rushed to market without thorough security testing. Hackers know this.

🔥 Common Security Weaknesses in EV Charging Stations

✘ Hardcoded credentials: Default admin passwords that never get changed.

✘ Unpatched firmware: Old software with known vulnerabilities.

✘ Lack of encryption: Data transmitted in plain text, ripe for interception.

✘ Weak authentication: Open ports and exposed APIs that allow remote access.

▢ How to Defend Against Attacks

✓ Use strong authentication mechanisms (OAuth, PKI, or multi-factor authentication).

✓ Encrypt communications using TLS 1.3 to prevent MITM attacks.

✓ Regularly update firmware to patch security flaws.

✓ Disable unnecessary network services that increase attack surface.

✓ Perform penetration testing on EV chargers before deployment.

▼ Case Study: In 2021, security researchers found that some public EV chargers had hardcoded admin passwords, allowing attackers to take complete control over the charging stations. That's like leaving your house keys taped to the front door.

2. Protecting V2G Networks from Cyber Attacks

Vehicle-to-grid (V2G) technology is an exciting innovation, allowing EVs to send electricity back to the grid when needed. But with great power comes great vulnerability—because now your car is an active part of the energy infrastructure.

🚨 Potential Cyber Threats in V2G Networks

Fake energy injection: Attackers trick the grid into thinking a vehicle is supplying power when it's not.

Load manipulation attacks: Hackers overload the grid by remotely controlling thousands of EVs.

Data spoofing: False charging data leads to incorrect billing or grid mismanagement.

Ransomware on V2G networks: Hackers could lock down charging networks and demand payment to restore service.

▢ Defensive Strategies for V2G Networks

✓ Implement strong cryptographic authentication between EVs and grid controllers.

✅ Use blockchain technology for secure energy transactions.

✅ Develop AI-driven anomaly detection to identify suspicious activity in real time.

✅ Ensure V2G systems use air-gapped or segmented networks to prevent lateral movement by attackers.

💡 **Industry Trend**: Some companies are now exploring zero-trust architecture for V2G, ensuring that no device or user is automatically trusted. This approach limits attack surfaces and prevents unauthorized access.

3. Strengthening Payment Security in EV Charging

EV charging transactions involve credit cards, mobile payments, and subscription-based billing—making them a juicy target for cybercriminals. Payment fraud is a real issue, with hackers exploiting poorly secured charging apps and backend payment gateways.

💳 Payment-Related Risks in EV Infrastructure
💳 Stolen credentials: Attackers intercept authentication tokens via MITM attacks.
📛 Fake charging stations: Fraudulent chargers steal credit card details.
📲 Mobile app exploits: Weak API security exposes payment data.

☐ How to Secure Payment Transactions

✅ Use tokenized payments to prevent direct exposure of credit card details.

✅ Enable two-factor authentication for charging accounts.

✅ Monitor transaction logs for unusual activity (e.g., repeated small charges).

✅ Adopt EMV chip & PIN standards for card-based charging transactions.

💡 **Tip**: If you use public EV chargers, avoid entering payment details on untrusted networks. Stick to secure apps and NFC-based transactions whenever possible.

4. Implementing AI and Machine Learning for EV Security

Let's face it—hackers are getting smarter. But so is security technology. AI and machine learning can help detect and prevent cyber threats in real-time.

How AI Enhances EV Charging Security

☐ Threat detection: AI can spot unusual patterns in charging sessions.

⚠ Anomaly detection: Identifies rogue devices on the network.

🔍 Predictive security: Anticipates attack patterns before they occur.

🔒 Automated response: AI-powered firewalls can block suspicious activity instantly.

💡 **Future Vision**: Imagine AI-driven cybersecurity agents that scan charging networks 24/7, automatically blocking cyber threats before they can cause damage. The tech exists—it just needs wider adoption.

Final Thoughts: The Road to a Secure EV Future

The EV revolution is unstoppable—but so are cybercriminals. Without strong security, EV charging networks and V2G systems are prime targets for attacks.

The good news? We know how to defend them. By enforcing strong encryption, secure authentication, AI-driven monitoring, and robust cybersecurity frameworks, we can ensure that EVs remain safe, reliable, and hacker-proof.

Because at the end of the day, charging your EV should be a smooth experience—not an open invitation for cybercriminals to drain your wallet or crash the power grid. So, let's build a future where EV security is as strong as its environmental promise.

🔌 Charge smart. Charge safe. And keep the hackers out. 🚗⚡💀

Chapter 9: Cyber-Physical Attacks and Blackout Scenarios

Imagine this: You're working from home, everything's running smoothly, when suddenly, the lights flicker and then—darkness. Your computer shuts off, your phone loses its connection, and the hum of your neighborhood is replaced by an eerie silence. You think it's just a random outage… until you hear rumors that the whole city is down, all at once. Now, add a sinister twist: a cyber attack has just taken control of the physical infrastructure, sending your entire power grid into chaos. This chapter brings you to the heart of one of the most terrifying scenarios in modern cybersecurity: the cyber-physical attack. We'll dive into how hackers can cause mayhem by targeting the very systems that control our physical world—like power plants, transformers, and distribution networks— and how such an attack could trigger a blackout that impacts millions. Ready for a deep dive into how digital and physical worlds collide with catastrophic results?

This chapter focuses on the intersection of cyber and physical security within critical infrastructure systems, particularly the power grid. Cyber-physical attacks represent one of the most complex and dangerous threats to modern infrastructure, where cyber intrusions are used to manipulate or damage physical assets, leading to widespread disruptions. We will explore how attackers can exploit vulnerabilities in control systems, such as SCADA (Supervisory Control and Data Acquisition) systems, to gain control over power plants, transformers, and other critical equipment. Through case studies and real-world scenarios, we will analyze the potential for large-scale blackouts, highlighting the risks posed by coordinated cyber-physical attacks. Finally, we will discuss strategies for preventing and mitigating these attacks, including robust system defenses, real-time monitoring, and incident response protocols, to safeguard our energy systems against catastrophic failures.

9.1 Understanding Cyber-Physical Risks in Smart Grid Systems

Alright, let's talk about cyber-physical risks in smart grids—because, let's face it, what's more exciting than the possibility of hackers causing actual blackouts? If you've ever wondered what happens when cybersecurity meets real-world power systems, you're in for a ride.

Smart grids are like the brain and nervous system of modern energy infrastructure—they monitor, automate, and optimize power generation and distribution. But here's the kicker: they are deeply connected to the internet, and you know what that means—hackers see them as a prime target. One well-placed cyber attack, and BOOM! Lights out.

So, let's break down how cyber threats can lead to real-world disasters, what's at stake, and how we can protect our power systems from digital mayhem.

The Cyber-Physical Nature of Smart Grids

Smart grids are not just about data and software; they directly control physical infrastructure like power plants, substations, and transformers. That's what makes them a cyber-physical system (CPS)—a network where digital commands translate into real-world actions.

🔲 Why is this a Big Deal?

A cyber attack on a bank may steal money, but a cyber attack on a smart grid can shut down an entire city.

Unlike traditional IT systems, smart grids deal with physics—power surges, overloads, and blackouts.

Compromising grid control systems can damage physical equipment, disrupt industries, and even threaten lives.

In simple terms, a hacked power grid isn't just an inconvenience—it's a national security threat.

Types of Cyber-Physical Risks in Smart Grid Systems

Now, let's dive into the real risks lurking in smart grids.

1. Grid Manipulation Attacks ⚡💀

Attackers can alter voltage levels, cause frequency instabilities, or overload power lines to physically damage equipment. This can trigger widespread blackouts or even permanent damage to critical infrastructure.

◈ **Example**: In 2015, Russian hackers took down parts of Ukraine's power grid using malware called BlackEnergy, leaving thousands without electricity.

◈ **Potential Consequence**: A well-executed grid manipulation attack could fry transformers, causing months-long outages.

☐ **Defense:**

✓ Use intrusion detection systems (IDS) to detect unauthorized changes.

✓ Implement automated fail-safes to isolate compromised sections.

2. SCADA & ICS Exploits 🏭

Supervisory Control and Data Acquisition (SCADA) and Industrial Control Systems (ICS) manage power generation and distribution. Unfortunately, many of these systems were designed decades ago, with zero security in mind.

◈ **Example**: Stuxnet, the infamous worm that sabotaged Iran's nuclear program by manipulating centrifuge speeds—proof that ICS exploits can cause real-world destruction.

◈ **Potential Consequence**: Hackers could alter power distribution, shut down substations, or even damage power plants.

☐ **Defense:**

✓ Update legacy systems and patch known vulnerabilities.

✓ Use network segmentation to prevent lateral movement.

3. IoT-Based Attacks on Smart Grid Devices ☐ 🔌

Smart grids rely on millions of IoT devices—smart meters, sensors, and connected transformers. But here's the problem: IoT devices are notorious for weak security.

◈ **Example**: In 2020, researchers discovered vulnerabilities in smart meters that allowed hackers to manipulate electricity usage data—potentially leading to billing fraud or grid instability.

◆ **Potential Consequence**: Attackers could turn off thousands of smart meters, causing a localized blackout or grid overload.

☐ **Defense:**

✓ Implement strong authentication for IoT devices.

✓ Regularly update firmware and remove default passwords.

4. Supply Chain Attacks on Grid Components ☐

The smart grid is built with hardware and software from dozens of vendors worldwide—and that's a security nightmare. If a single component is compromised during manufacturing or distribution, the entire grid can be at risk.

◆ **Example**: In 2021, the SolarWinds attack showed how a supply chain compromise could infiltrate critical infrastructure undetected.

◆ **Potential Consequence**: Malicious firmware or backdoors in grid components could allow hackers persistent access to critical systems.

☐ **Defense:**

✓ Vet suppliers carefully and enforce security standards.

✓ Use hardware-based cryptographic validation to verify firmware integrity.

5. Ransomware Targeting Power Grids 💰🔒

Ransomware attacks have evolved from targeting corporate data to threatening critical infrastructure. A ransomware infection in a power utility's network can lock operators out of their own systems—demanding millions in ransom payments.

◆ **Example**: In 2021, the Colonial Pipeline ransomware attack disrupted fuel supplies across the U.S., showing how critical infrastructure is vulnerable to cyber extortion.

◆ **Potential Consequence**: Ransomware in a smart grid could halt power distribution, disrupt industries, and endanger public safety.

☐ Defense:

✅ Regularly back up critical grid control data.

✅ Implement network segmentation to prevent ransomware spread.

Mitigating Cyber-Physical Risks in Smart Grids

Now that we know the threats, how do we protect smart grids from cyber-physical attacks?

☐ 1. Zero Trust Architecture

Never assume any device or user is trusted.

Require continuous authentication and least privilege access.

☐ 2. AI-Powered Anomaly Detection

Use machine learning to detect abnormal grid behavior.

Automate threat detection and response to minimize attack impact.

☐ 3. Stronger Encryption & Authentication

Implement end-to-end encryption in grid communications.

Require multi-factor authentication (MFA) for all control systems.

☐ 4. Regular Cyber Drills & Penetration Testing

Simulate cyber-physical attack scenarios to test grid resilience.

Identify and patch vulnerabilities before real hackers exploit them.

Final Thoughts: Powering Up Smart Grid Security

If there's one thing to take away from this, it's this: cybersecurity in smart grids isn't just about protecting data—it's about protecting power, safety, and national security.

A cyber-physical attack on an energy grid isn't just an IT problem—it's an entire nation's problem. The good news? We have the tools, strategies, and technology to defend against these threats.

So, let's build a future where smart grids are not just smart—but also secure. Because the only blackout we want to see is when we turn off the lights by choice. ☺

9.2 Grid Manipulation Attacks and Large-Scale Power Disruptions

Alright, let's get real—what's more terrifying than a hacker in a hoodie? A hacker in a hoodie who just took down your entire city's power grid! Imagine scrolling through social media, then—bam!—your screen goes black, your fridge stops humming, and the only light in sight is your neighbor's emergency candles.

This isn't a plot from a dystopian thriller; it's a very real cybersecurity nightmare. Grid manipulation attacks are some of the most devastating cyber-physical threats because they don't just mess with computers—they shut down entire power infrastructures. And the worst part? Attackers don't need explosives or an army—just a laptop, an internet connection, and some knowledge of industrial control systems (ICS).

Let's dive into how hackers can manipulate the grid, what damage they can cause, and most importantly—how we can fight back.

What Are Grid Manipulation Attacks?

A grid manipulation attack is when a hacker gains access to the power grid's control systems and deliberately alters power flow, voltage levels, or grid operations. Unlike a traditional cyber attack that focuses on stealing data, this type of attack is about causing physical consequences—like shutting down power stations or overloading transformers.

🔓 What Can Hackers Do?

Trigger blackouts by shutting down power plants remotely.

Cause voltage fluctuations that damage industrial and consumer electronics.

Overload power lines, potentially leading to fires or equipment failure.

Disable protective systems, making the grid vulnerable to cascading failures.

These attacks don't just affect businesses—they disrupt hospitals, emergency services, water supply systems, and even financial markets.

Real-World Examples of Grid Manipulation Attacks

Unfortunately, this isn't just theory—we've already seen grid attacks play out in the real world.

1. The Ukraine Power Grid Attack (2015 & 2016) ⚡

What Happened? Russian hackers used a malware called BlackEnergy to infiltrate Ukraine's power grid. They took remote control of substations and shut down power to over 230,000 people in the middle of winter.

Impact: A well-coordinated cyber attack left entire regions in the dark for hours.

Takeaway: Attackers didn't destroy the grid—they just turned it off, proving that remote sabotage is possible.

2. Stuxnet and the Lessons for Power Grids 🏭

What Happened? Stuxnet, the infamous cyber weapon, was designed to sabotage Iran's nuclear program by manipulating centrifuge speeds.

Impact: Though it targeted nuclear systems, it showed how industrial control systems (ICS) could be hacked to cause physical destruction—a method applicable to power grids.

3. The Colonial Pipeline Ransomware Attack (2021) ⛽

What Happened? A ransomware attack forced the shutdown of a major fuel pipeline in the U.S., showing how cyber threats can have real-world consequences.

Takeaway: The attack didn't directly target the grid, but it demonstrated how critical infrastructure is vulnerable to cyber extortion.

If these attacks taught us anything, it's that the grid isn't just a network of wires and transformers—it's a battleground.

How Hackers Manipulate the Grid

So, how do attackers actually take control of power infrastructure? Here are some of the most common methods.

1. Exploiting Industrial Control Systems (ICS) & SCADA

Most power grids rely on Supervisory Control and Data Acquisition (SCADA) systems to monitor and control grid components. The problem? Many SCADA systems were built before cybersecurity was a priority—meaning they often lack encryption, authentication, and proper access controls.

◆ **Attack Strategy:**

Hackers use phishing emails or exposed credentials to gain remote access.

They send malicious commands to shut down power stations or alter voltage levels.

☐ **Defense:**

✓ Implement multi-factor authentication (MFA) for all grid operators.

✓ Upgrade legacy SCADA systems with modern security controls.

2. Man-in-the-Middle (MITM) Attacks on Grid Communications

Power grid components communicate using protocols like DNP3, IEC 61850, and Modbus—but many of these lack encryption! This makes them a prime target for MITM attacks, where hackers intercept and alter grid commands.

◆ **Attack Strategy:**

Intercept communication between a power station and its control center.

Inject fake commands to disable safety mechanisms or manipulate power flow.

☐ **Defense:**

✓ Use end-to-end encryption for grid communications.

✓ Deploy anomaly detection systems to catch unusual network activity.

3. Targeting IoT and Smart Grid Devices

Smart meters, sensors, and automated distribution devices are all connected to the grid—and many have weak default security settings. A compromised IoT device could act as a backdoor into the grid's network.

◆ **Attack Strategy:**

Hackers infect thousands of smart meters with malware.

They remotely disconnect meters from the grid, causing localized outages.

☐ **Defense:**

✓ Use strong encryption and authentication for all IoT devices.

✓ Regularly update firmware and remove default passwords.

The Consequences of a Large-Scale Power Disruption
Grid manipulation attacks don't just turn off the lights—they cripple entire economies. Here's what's at stake:

🔥 **Economic Impact:**

A single large-scale blackout can cause billions in damages.

Businesses, factories, and banks lose productivity and revenue.

🚑 **Public Safety Risks:**

Hospitals lose life-saving equipment without backup power.

Traffic lights go dark, leading to chaos on the roads.

💻 **Cyber Warfare & National Security:**

Grid attacks are a favorite tool of nation-state hackers.

A successful attack can be used to destabilize governments.

Defending Against Grid Manipulation Attacks

Here's how we keep the lights on and hackers out:

☐ **1. Network Segmentation & Zero Trust Security**

Separate grid control networks from the public internet.

Implement Zero Trust principles—never assume any device is secure.

☐ **2. AI-Based Grid Monitoring & Threat Detection**

Use machine learning algorithms to detect unusual grid behavior.

Automate responses to block malicious activity in real-time.

☐ **3. Regular Cyber Drills & Incident Response Plans**

Simulate grid attack scenarios to test response readiness.

Train operators to detect and respond to cyber threats quickly.

Final Thoughts: Keeping the Power On in a Cyber War

At the end of the day, the smart grid is only as smart as its security. Attackers are constantly evolving their tactics, so we need to stay ahead of the game.

The next big cyber war won't be fought with tanks and missiles—it'll be fought in the shadows, through code and power grids. But with the right defensive strategies, technology, and vigilance, we can make sure that when the next attack comes, the only blackout happening is in the hacker's basement. 💡☺

9.3 Exploiting Renewable Energy Systems and Microgrids

Alright, picture this: You just installed a fancy new solar panel system on your roof, and now you feel like Tony Stark, generating your own electricity. But guess what? That sleek, eco-friendly tech you just set up might be a goldmine for hackers.

Renewable energy systems and microgrids are becoming essential parts of the modern power grid, but with great power (literally) comes great cybersecurity risks. Whether it's solar farms, wind turbines, or decentralized energy storage, these systems are highly connected, often rely on IoT and remote management, and—here's the kicker—many are poorly secured.

If a hacker wants to manipulate energy prices, disrupt power flow, or even cause cascading grid failures, renewable energy systems and microgrids are prime targets. Let's dive into how they can be exploited and, more importantly, how to stop them.

What Are Renewable Energy Systems and Microgrids?

☐ **Renewable Energy Systems**

These include:

✅ **Solar power systems** (rooftop panels, solar farms, battery storage)
✅ **Wind energy systems** (onshore and offshore wind farms)
✅ Hydropower and geothermal systems

All of these rely on smart inverters, IoT sensors, and remote connectivity, which means they introduce new attack surfaces to the grid.

⚡ **Microgrids: The Grid's Backup Plan**

A microgrid is a localized energy system that can function independently or connect to the main power grid. It's like having your own mini-power station that keeps the lights on even if the main grid fails.

Microgrids are often used in:

✅ **Hospitals** (critical power backup)
✅ **Military bases** (energy resilience)
✅ Smart cities and remote areas

While microgrids add flexibility and resilience to the energy sector, they also increase cybersecurity risks by introducing more points of entry for attackers.

How Hackers Exploit Renewable Energy Systems and Microgrids

1. Hacking Smart Inverters and Grid-Tied Systems

Modern renewable energy systems rely on smart inverters to convert DC power into AC and manage power flow. These inverters are often connected to the internet for remote monitoring. You see where this is going, right?

◆ **Attack Strategy:**

Hackers exploit default passwords or unpatched vulnerabilities in inverter firmware.

They remotely shut down or alter the output of solar/wind systems.

Mass inverter manipulation could destabilize the grid by suddenly reducing power supply.

☐ **Defense:**

✓ Change default passwords on all inverters.

✓ Regularly update firmware and patch vulnerabilities.

✓ Use network segmentation to isolate inverters from the internet.

2. Manipulating Energy Storage Systems (Batteries & Virtual Power Plants)

Battery storage systems (like Tesla Powerwalls or industrial-scale battery farms) allow users to store excess energy and sell it back to the grid. But what if hackers could remotely drain or overload these systems?

◆ **Attack Strategy:**

Hackers exploit API vulnerabilities in cloud-based energy management platforms.

They trigger a mass battery discharge, causing sudden power instability.

Attackers fake energy production reports, manipulating energy markets.

☐ Defense:

✅ Secure API connections with strong authentication and encryption.

✅ Monitor for suspicious battery discharge patterns.

✅ Implement failsafe controls to prevent forced discharges.

3. Compromising Wind Turbine Control Systems

Wind farms rely on remote telemetry and industrial control systems (ICS) to operate efficiently. Unfortunately, many wind turbines still use legacy ICS protocols (like Modbus, DNP3, or unencrypted TCP connections) that hackers love to exploit.

◆ Attack Strategy:

Hackers gain remote access to a wind farm's control center.

They alter turbine speeds or disable braking systems, leading to mechanical failure.

Attackers reverse power output, disrupting grid stability.

☐ Defense:

✅ Use encrypted communication for wind farm telemetry.

✅ Apply intrusion detection systems (IDS) to detect unauthorized control changes.

✅ Regularly audit ICS access controls.

4. Microgrid Takeover: The Ultimate Power Grab

Microgrids rely on distributed energy resources (DERs), which are often managed remotely. If a hacker gains control, they can:

Cut off power to critical infrastructure.

Redirect energy flows, overloading local transformers.

Create a cascading failure, destabilizing the main grid.

◆ Attack Strategy:

Hackers target poorly secured microgrid controllers.

They spoof energy demand data, forcing microgrids into overproduction or shutdown.

Attackers disable backup generators, leading to power loss.

☐ Defense:

✓ Secure microgrid controllers with MFA and network segmentation.

✓ Deploy real-time anomaly detection for energy flow patterns.

✓ Implement physical security for key microgrid control centers.

The Big Picture: Why This Matters

If attackers successfully exploit renewable energy systems and microgrids, the consequences could be devastating:

🔥 Economic & Grid Stability Risks:

Mass inverter shutdowns could cause sudden energy shortages.

Energy market manipulation could lead to huge financial losses.

🚨 National Security Risks:

Hackers could weaponize the energy grid in cyber warfare scenarios.

Attackers could cripple emergency services by shutting down microgrids.

☐ Environmental & Social Impacts:

A compromised renewable system damages public trust in clean energy.

Grid failures can lead to widespread chaos and infrastructure damage.

How to Strengthen Security in Renewable Energy and Microgrids

🔒 1. Adopt Zero Trust Security for Energy Systems

Never assume any device or user is trustworthy by default.

Require multi-factor authentication (MFA) for all control systems.

📢 2. Encrypt All Communications

Use end-to-end encryption for smart inverters and microgrid controllers.

Avoid legacy ICS protocols without security enhancements.

🚀 3. Deploy AI-Based Threat Detection

AI can detect anomalies in energy usage and grid performance.

Automated response systems can shut down threats before damage occurs.

🔧 4. Regular Security Audits & Penetration Testing

Continuously test for vulnerabilities in renewable energy systems.

Patch firmware before attackers exploit known weaknesses.

Final Thoughts: Can We Hack-Proof Renewable Energy?

The future of energy is renewable, decentralized, and smart—but that also means it's more exposed to cyber threats than ever before. Hackers aren't just going after banks or social media accounts anymore. They're coming for the power that runs our homes, hospitals, and cities.

The good news? With proper cybersecurity practices, we can keep our renewable energy systems resilient. Because let's be honest—solar panels should be soaking up the sun, not getting hacked by some guy in his basement. ☀️🔲😆

9.4 Case Studies: Stuxnet, Industroyer, and BlackEnergy Attacks

Alright, folks—time for a little cyber horror story session. No jump scares, just real-world cyberattacks that have messed with power grids, industrial control systems (ICS), and critical infrastructure in ways that sound like a sci-fi thriller.

Stuxnet, Industroyer, and BlackEnergy aren't just fancy hacker names—they're some of the most notorious cyber weapons ever unleashed. These attacks didn't just steal data or crash websites; they physically damaged equipment, shut down power grids, and changed the way cybersecurity experts think about digital warfare.

Let's break them down, figure out how they worked, and see what lessons we can learn before the next big attack happens.

☢☐ Stuxnet: The Cyber Weapon That Took Down Nuclear Centrifuges

Imagine you're an engineer running a nuclear plant. One day, everything looks fine on your control panel, but in reality, your machines are spinning out of control, and you don't even know it. That's Stuxnet in a nutshell.

What Happened?

Stuxnet was a sophisticated worm discovered in 2010.

It specifically targeted Siemens PLCs (Programmable Logic Controllers) used in Iran's Natanz nuclear facility.

The malware altered the speed of uranium centrifuges, causing them to self-destruct, all while displaying normal readings to operators.

How It Worked

Initial Infection: It spread via USB drives—no internet connection required.

Zero-Day Exploits: It used four zero-day vulnerabilities (rare at the time).

PLC Manipulation: Once inside, it reprogrammed Siemens PLCs to alter centrifuge speeds.

Stealth Mode: Operators saw fake normal readings, so they had no idea equipment was failing.

Lessons Learned

✓ Air-gapped systems aren't invincible—Stuxnet bypassed internet isolation.

✓ Supply chain security matters—Stuxnet spread through infected third-party software.

✓ Industrial systems need real-time anomaly detection—Normal-looking data can be fake.

Stuxnet redefined cyber warfare, proving that malware can cause real-world destruction, not just data breaches.

⚡ Industroyer: The Cyberattack That Shut Down a Power Grid

Fast forward to 2016. It's a cold December night in Ukraine when suddenly—lights out. The capital Kyiv lost power for over an hour, thanks to one of the most sophisticated cyberattacks ever seen: Industroyer.

What Happened?

Industroyer specifically targeted Ukraine's power grid, taking down substations.

It was the first known malware built to control industrial circuit breakers directly.

The attack was highly automated, requiring minimal human intervention.

How It Worked

Compromised Networks: Hackers gained access months before the attack.

Custom Malware Modules: Industroyer could speak multiple ICS protocols (IEC 61850, OPC DA, etc.).

Breaker Manipulation: The malware sent signals to open circuit breakers, shutting down power.

Self-Destruction: After doing its job, Industroyer wiped traces of itself.

Lessons Learned

✅ SCADA systems should never be directly accessible from corporate networks.

✅ Legacy ICS protocols lack authentication—attackers can send unauthorized commands.

✅ Regular security monitoring and threat hunting are critical to detecting silent intrusions.

Industroyer wasn't just an attack—it was a warning shot. If attackers could do this to Ukraine, they could do it anywhere.

🔲🔲 BlackEnergy: The Trojan That Took Down Ukraine's Power Grid (Again!)

Before Industroyer, there was BlackEnergy—the first known cyberattack that took down a power grid. If Industroyer was a sniper shot, BlackEnergy was a sledgehammer.

What Happened?

In 2015, Ukraine's power grid was hit, causing a 6-hour blackout for 225,000 people.

The attack started months before, with phishing emails sent to power companies.

It was a multi-stage attack, using BlackEnergy malware to gain control of SCADA systems.

How It Worked

Phishing Emails: Employees received emails with infected Word documents.

Backdoor Access: Once opened, malware installed a backdoor for remote control.

SCADA Control Hijacked: Attackers gained access to power distribution substations.

Manual Shutdowns: Hackers remotely opened circuit breakers, cutting off electricity.

Lessons Learned

✓ Employees need cybersecurity training—phishing can take down entire power grids.

✓ Firewalls and segmentation could have prevented SCADA access from IT networks.

✓ Incident response drills should prepare for coordinated cyber-physical attacks.

BlackEnergy showed that cyberattacks don't need fancy zero-day exploits—human mistakes can be just as effective.

☐ What Can We Learn from These Attacks?

1. Critical Infrastructure is a Prime Target

Cybercriminals, nation-state hackers, and terrorists see power grids as high-value targets.

These attacks weren't for fun—they were deliberate acts of cyber warfare.

2. Air-Gapped Systems Aren't Safe

Stuxnet showed that even offline systems can be compromised.

Attackers use USB drives, insider threats, and supply chain vulnerabilities.

3. ICS Protocols Were Never Designed for Security

Many industrial control systems lack authentication and encryption.

Attackers can send direct control commands once they gain access.

4. Cyber-Physical Attacks Have Real-World Consequences

These aren't just computer viruses—they cause blackouts, equipment damage, and even geopolitical crises.

🚨 Final Thoughts: Are We Ready for the Next Attack?

Let's be real—we're not.

Attacks like Stuxnet, Industroyer, and BlackEnergy exposed massive vulnerabilities in the way we secure power grids. And let's be honest, we haven't completely fixed them yet.

With the rise of IoT, AI-driven automation, and smart grids, the attack surface is getting bigger every day. If hackers were able to shut down power grids a decade ago, imagine what they could do now with AI-powered malware and 5G-enabled cyber weapons.

The question isn't if another attack will happen. It's when.

So, whether you're a security pro, an energy grid operator, or just someone who enjoys having electricity, now's the time to start taking cybersecurity seriously. Because trust me, reading in the dark isn't fun. 🔦😅

9.5 Building Resilient Smart Grid Defenses Against Cyber Threats

Alright, let's be real—cybercriminals, state-sponsored hackers, and even script kiddies with too much time on their hands love the idea of messing with the power grid. Why? Because it's one of the most critical infrastructures on the planet. Knock out the grid, and you create chaos—no lights, no internet, no Netflix (a true nightmare).

But while attackers are always leveling up, so are we. Defending the smart grid isn't about just slapping on some firewalls and hoping for the best. It's about building layered, resilient security that can withstand even the nastiest cyber onslaughts. So, let's break down how we can turn our smart grid into a cyber fortress.

🔒 The Cybersecurity Triad: Prevention, Detection, and Response

Resilience isn't just about blocking attacks—it's about detecting and recovering from them too. Smart grid security needs to be built on three key pillars:

Prevention – Stop attacks before they happen.

Detection – Identify breaches early.

Response & Recovery – Minimize damage and restore operations fast.

Let's see how each of these works in practice.

🛡 Prevention: Hardening the Smart Grid Against Attacks

1️⃣ Network Segmentation: Keeping IT and OT Separate

One of the biggest mistakes utilities make is mixing IT (Information Technology) and OT (Operational Technology) networks. Attackers love this because once they breach the corporate IT network, they can waltz right into the SCADA system.

✅ Use firewalls, VLANs, and air gaps to isolate critical infrastructure.

✅ Apply Zero Trust principles—assume every connection is a potential threat.

✅ Regularly audit remote access points to ensure only authorized personnel get in.

2️⃣ Secure Authentication and Access Control

Your grid's security is only as strong as your weakest password. Attackers often use stolen or weak credentials to slip into networks.

✅ Implement multi-factor authentication (MFA)—especially for critical systems.

✅ Use role-based access control (RBAC)—not everyone should have admin privileges.

✅ Monitor user activity logs for suspicious access attempts.

3️⃣ Patch Management and Vulnerability Mitigation

Many ICS and SCADA systems still run on outdated software because companies fear downtime. But guess what? Hackers love unpatched vulnerabilities.

✅ Regularly update and patch industrial control system firmware.

✅ Use virtual patching if updating isn't immediately possible.

✅ Perform routine vulnerability assessments to spot weaknesses before attackers do.

🔍 Detection: Finding the Attack Before It's Too Late

4️⃣ Intrusion Detection Systems (IDS) and Network Monitoring

You can't stop an attack if you don't know it's happening. That's why real-time monitoring is critical.

✅ Deploy Intrusion Detection/Prevention Systems (IDS/IPS) in IT and OT networks.

✅ Use behavioral analytics to detect unusual activity (e.g., a control system suddenly sending rogue commands).

✅ Monitor logs from SCADA, AMI, and EMS systems to identify anomalies.

5️⃣ AI and Machine Learning for Threat Detection

Attackers are getting smarter, but so are our defenses. AI-powered cybersecurity tools can detect patterns of cyber threats before they escalate.

✅ Use AI-based anomaly detection to flag suspicious activity.

✅ Implement machine learning-driven log analysis to spot hidden attacks.

✅ Train AI models with historical cyberattack data for better threat prediction.

🚨 Response and Recovery: Minimizing Damage and Restoring Operations

6️⃣ Incident Response Plans: Preparing for the Worst

When a cyberattack happens (and it will), a well-prepared response plan can mean the difference between a minor disruption and a nationwide blackout.

✅ Create a detailed Incident Response (IR) plan for handling cyberattacks.

✅ Run regular tabletop exercises simulating real-world attacks.

✅ Define clear roles and responsibilities—who does what when things go south?

7️⃣ Backup and Disaster Recovery Strategies

If ransomware locks up your grid's control systems, do you have a clean backup ready?

✅ Regularly back up configurations and critical data offline.

✅ Use immutable backups that can't be modified or encrypted by attackers.

✅ Test recovery procedures frequently to ensure they actually work.

⚡ The Role of AI and Automation in Smart Grid Defense

Cybersecurity teams are outnumbered—there are way more attackers than defenders. This is where AI and automation come in.

✅ Automated threat hunting can identify cyber threats in real-time.

✅ AI-powered predictive analytics can warn utilities before an attack occurs.

✅ Automated patch management ensures critical updates aren't ignored.

Think of it as having a tireless cybersecurity assistant that never sleeps, never takes coffee breaks, and doesn't get fooled by phishing emails.

🏆 Future-Proofing the Smart Grid: What's Next?

Cyber threats will only get more advanced. To stay ahead, smart grid security needs to keep evolving.

🔮 Upcoming Trends in Smart Grid Cybersecurity

Quantum cryptography for unbreakable encryption.

Blockchain-based security to prevent data tampering.

AI-powered cyber defense teams that learn from every attack.

Utilities must invest in cybersecurity now, before they become the next case study in a cybersecurity horror story.

🖊 Final Thoughts: Let's Not Be the Next Headline

The last thing any of us want is to wake up to a massive blackout caused by hackers. But if history has taught us anything (hello, Stuxnet and Industroyer), it's that attackers love critical infrastructure.

The smart grid is an incredible innovation, but without strong security, it's also a massive attack surface. It's up to us—security professionals, engineers, and policymakers—to harden the grid, detect threats early, and respond effectively.

Because let's be honest—if the hackers win, the only thing we'll be charging is our candles. 🔦😄

Chapter 10: Defending and Hardening the Smart Grid

So, we've talked about all the ways the bad guys can exploit the vulnerabilities in our smart grids—from hijacking EV charging stations to messing with edge computing. But what happens when the cyber villains meet the heroes of cybersecurity? It's time to fight back! Just like any great story, this chapter flips the script. We're not here to just sit back and wait for the next attack—we're arming ourselves with the tools, strategies, and know-how to lock down the smart grid and keep the hackers at bay. From patching up weak spots to deploying advanced defensive measures, this is the playbook you need to harden the grid and ensure its resilience against all kinds of threats. Grab your cybersecurity cape; it's time to power up the defenses!

In this chapter, we delve into the best practices and technical approaches for defending and hardening smart grid systems against a wide array of cyber threats. As critical infrastructure becomes more interconnected and reliant on digital technologies, ensuring its security is paramount to maintaining the stability and reliability of the power grid. We will examine a multi-layered defense strategy that includes everything from network segmentation and encryption to advanced intrusion detection systems (IDS) and real-time monitoring. Additionally, we'll discuss the importance of regular updates, rigorous testing, and continuous risk assessments to identify and address vulnerabilities before they can be exploited. By implementing these defense mechanisms, utilities and grid operators can bolster their systems against both external and internal threats, ensuring the continued operation and security of smart grid infrastructure in the face of evolving cyber risks.

10.1 Implementing Security Best Practices in Smart Grid Networks

Ah, security best practices—the magical checklist that every cybersecurity expert loves to preach, but so many organizations fail to follow. Why? Because securing the smart grid isn't as simple as slapping a firewall on it and calling it a day. It's a complex beast, a Frankenstein of IT (Information Technology) and OT (Operational Technology), with millions of devices, outdated systems, and some of the most persistent hackers on the planet trying to break in.

If you think your home Wi-Fi password is enough to keep the bad guys out of the smart grid, think again. This chapter is all about turning wishful thinking into actionable security measures. We're going to break down real, practical steps that make attackers' lives miserable and keep the lights on for everyone else.

☐☐ The Pillars of Smart Grid Security

Before we dive into the nitty-gritty, let's set the foundation. Smart grid security revolves around three main pillars:

1☐ **Confidentiality** – Keep critical energy data out of unauthorized hands.

2☐ **Integrity** – Prevent attackers from altering grid commands or meter readings.

3☐ **Availability** – Ensure power delivery continues, even under attack.

If any of these pillars crumble, the grid becomes vulnerable. So let's build a fortress, one security layer at a time.

☐ 1. Network Segmentation: Keep IT and OT Apart!

One of the biggest mistakes in smart grid security is allowing IT and OT networks to mingle too freely. Imagine letting office employees access the same network as critical control systems—it's like leaving your house keys at a hacker convention.

✓ Best Practices for Network Segmentation

✓☐ Use firewalls, VLANs, and DMZs to isolate IT from OT.
✓☐ Implement Zero Trust principles—assume no connection is safe.
✓☐ Enforce strict role-based access control (RBAC) to limit access.

By keeping IT and OT separate, we prevent hackers from pivoting from a phished corporate email straight into SCADA command centers.

☐ 2. Strong Authentication: Because Password123 Isn't Security

Attackers love weak passwords—and they really love when utilities still use default credentials like admin/admin.

✓ Best Practices for Authentication

✓☐ Enforce Multi-Factor Authentication (MFA) for all critical systems.

✓☐ Use strong, unique passwords—none of that "SmartGrid2024!" nonsense.

✓☐ Implement hardware security tokens for privileged accounts.

Let's make brute-force attacks and credential stuffing a hacker's worst nightmare.

🔍 3. Real-Time Monitoring and Intrusion Detection

Would you leave a bank vault unmonitored? No? Then why let your smart grid run without real-time threat detection?

✅ Best Practices for Threat Monitoring

✓☐ Deploy Intrusion Detection/Prevention Systems (IDS/IPS) to catch suspicious activity.

✓☐ Use AI-powered anomaly detection to spot threats before they escalate.

✓☐ Implement SIEM (Security Information and Event Management) for log correlation.

If a hacker breaches the grid, real-time monitoring helps you spot them before they do real damage.

☐☐ 4. Secure Firmware Updates and Patch Management

Ah, legacy systems—the Achilles' heel of smart grid security. Many ICS and SCADA systems are still running on decades-old firmware, full of vulnerabilities that hackers actively exploit.

✅ Best Practices for Patching & Firmware Security

✓☐ Implement secure, signed firmware updates to prevent tampering.

✓☐ Apply virtual patching when immediate updates aren't possible.

✓☐ Use AI-driven vulnerability scanners to identify weak spots.

A single unpatched device can become an entry point for an entire grid attack.

☐ 5. Implementing Red Team & Penetration Testing

You can't defend the smart grid if you don't know where it's weak. That's where red teaming and penetration testing come in.

✅ Best Practices for Smart Grid Penetration Testing

✓☐ Conduct regular red team exercises simulating real-world attacks.
✓☐ Test for physical security weaknesses—can an attacker just walk into a substation?
✓☐ Use automated and manual pentesting tools to uncover hidden flaws.

Finding vulnerabilities before attackers do is the key to staying ahead.

📜 6. Compliance Standards: Because Rules Exist for a Reason

No one likes compliance paperwork, but in smart grid security, it saves lives.

✅ Key Compliance Standards for Smart Grid Security

✓☐ **NERC CIP** (North American Electric Reliability Corporation Critical Infrastructure Protection) – Mandatory for power utilities.
✓☐ **IEC 62443** – Essential for industrial control system security.
✓☐ **ISO 27019** – Focuses on securing energy infrastructure.

Compliance isn't just a checkbox exercise—it helps prevent catastrophic failures.

📟 7. Incident Response: Because You Can't Stop Every Attack

Even with the best security in place, attacks will happen. A well-prepared Incident Response Plan (IRP) can minimize damage and restore operations quickly.

✅ Best Practices for Smart Grid Incident Response

✓☐ Define clear roles—who does what when an attack occurs?
✓☐ Establish cyber forensics procedures to investigate breaches.
✓☐ Run regular cybersecurity drills simulating ransomware, DDoS, and intrusion attempts.

A well-executed response can turn a potential blackout into a minor inconvenience.

⚡ Future-Proofing: What's Next in Smart Grid Security?

Cyber threats aren't slowing down, and neither can we.

⦿ Future Trends in Smart Grid Security

✓ **AI-driven cybersecurity** – Smarter threat detection with machine learning.
✓ **Quantum encryption** – Unbreakable security for grid communications.
✓ **Blockchain-based security** – Secure, tamper-proof transactions for energy trading.

The future of smart grid security is evolving, and staying ahead of the curve isn't optional—it's a necessity.

🖊 Final Thoughts: Securing the Grid is a Team Effort

The smart grid is an amazing technological achievement, but it also comes with massive security risks. One bad breach, and we're all stuck in the dark, living like it's the 1800s again (no Wi-Fi, no coffee makers, pure horror).

But here's the good news: we can secure it. By implementing layered defenses, proactive monitoring, and strong response strategies, we can build a resilient, cyber-proof energy grid.

So, let's lock it down—because the only thing that should be getting hacked is your neighbor's terrible smart fridge that keeps ordering pineapples by mistake. 🍍😄

10.2 Real-Time Monitoring and Anomaly Detection for Grid Security

You know that feeling when your Wi-Fi suddenly slows down, and you suspect your neighbor is secretly streaming 4K movies on your network? Now imagine that happening on a national power grid level—except instead of Netflix bandwidth hogs, it's cybercriminals manipulating energy distribution, causing outages, or siphoning off sensitive data. Yeah, not great.

That's where real-time monitoring and anomaly detection come in. Instead of waiting for a catastrophic failure (or a ransom demand from some hacker in a basement), these tools help spot unusual activity before disaster strikes. It's like having a cybersecurity guard dog—except it doesn't need snacks and doesn't bark at the mailman.

👀 Why Real-Time Monitoring Matters in Smart Grid Security

The smart grid is a massive, interconnected system, blending IT (Information Technology) and OT (Operational Technology). It's got smart meters, SCADA systems, IoT sensors, industrial controllers, and communication networks all talking to each other—making it a prime target for cyber threats.

Real-time monitoring acts as the watchtower, continuously scanning for:

✓ Unauthorized access attempts (a hacker probing for weaknesses)

✓ Data inconsistencies (meter readings suddenly doubling overnight)

✓ Abnormal traffic patterns (massive data transfers that shouldn't happen)

✓ Device misbehavior (smart meters suddenly sending weird signals)

With anomaly detection, we can spot these threats before they turn into full-blown cyberattacks.

☐ Common Smart Grid Anomalies and Their Risks

🔥 1. Sudden Spikes in Energy Demand

Imagine a small neighborhood suddenly consuming as much power as an industrial city. Either aliens landed and set up shop, or someone is trying to manipulate the grid.

☞ **Risk**: This could be a meter data injection attack, where hackers alter power consumption reports to commit billing fraud or overload grid components.

🖬 2. Unusual Network Traffic Patterns

A substation usually sends X amount of data per day. Suddenly, it's transmitting 100X the normal amount. Either the power company started a TikTok channel (unlikely) or someone is exfiltrating critical grid data.

☞ **Risk**: This could be an exfiltration attack, where an attacker steals sensitive operational data or launches a denial-of-service (DoS) attack.

⚡ 3. Remote Commands from Unauthorized Sources

Grid operators have strictly controlled access, but suddenly, a command comes from an unknown IP, telling a substation to shut down. That's like getting an email from "Prince of Nigeria" asking for your passwords.

☞ **Risk**: This is a sign of MITM (Man-in-the-Middle) attacks or unauthorized access, where attackers manipulate grid operations.

☐☠☐ 4. Devices Sending Data at Odd Hours

SCADA systems usually communicate on predictable schedules. If devices start sending data at 3 AM, either the grid is haunted, or someone's tampering with industrial control systems.

☞ **Risk**: Could indicate malware, a compromised device, or a botnet preparing for an attack.

🔍 Tools and Techniques for Smart Grid Monitoring

☐☐ 1. Intrusion Detection and Prevention Systems (IDS/IPS)

Think of this as a home security system, but for the grid. IDS monitors all traffic for suspicious activity, while IPS takes it a step further by blocking threats automatically.

✅ Best Practices:

✓ Deploy network-based IDS for large-scale monitoring

✓ Use host-based IDS to protect individual grid devices

✓ Train IDS with AI models for better detection of new threats

☐ 2. AI and Machine Learning for Anomaly Detection

Humans are great, but machines don't need coffee breaks. AI-driven systems analyze patterns and detect subtle anomalies that humans might miss.

✅ Best Practices:

✓ Use unsupervised learning models to identify unknown threats

✓ Train ML models on historical attack data to improve accuracy

✓ Implement adaptive security—systems that adjust based on real-time threats

□□♂□ 3. Security Information and Event Management (SIEM) Systems

SIEM tools collect logs from all smart grid components, analyze them, and raise alerts for suspicious activity. It's like having a detective piecing together cybercrime evidence in real time.

✅ Best Practices:

✓ Correlate SCADA, AMI, and IT logs for a unified security view

✓ Set up automated alerts for unusual activity

✓ Use behavior analytics to detect insider threats

🔑 4. Zero Trust Security Model

The old-school security model assumed everything inside the network was safe—which is why hackers love breaking in. Zero Trust assumes nothing is safe.

✅ Best Practices:

✓ Require multi-factor authentication (MFA) everywhere

✓ Use micro-segmentation to isolate grid components

✓ Monitor every access request, even from internal users

□ Challenges in Implementing Real-Time Monitoring

1. Too Many False Positives

Anomaly detection can sometimes be like that overcautious friend who thinks every noise in the house is a ghost. Too many false alerts lead to alarm fatigue, making teams ignore real threats.

☐ Solution:

✓ Use AI-powered filtering to reduce false positives

✓ Fine-tune alert thresholds to avoid unnecessary panic

2. Legacy Systems with Limited Security Features

Some smart grid components were built before cybersecurity was even a concern (looking at you, decades-old SCADA systems).

☐ Solution:

✓ Use security gateways to protect legacy devices

✓ Deploy virtual patching to fix vulnerabilities when updates aren't available

⚡ 3. Balancing Security with System Performance

Too much monitoring can slow down smart grid operations—kind of like installing too many antivirus programs on a computer.

☐ Solution:

✓ Optimize data collection intervals to avoid overload

✓ Use edge computing to analyze threats locally before sending data to the cloud

🔊 Final Thoughts: Stay Vigilant, Stay Secure!

Cyber threats to the smart grid aren't going away—in fact, they're getting more sophisticated. But with real-time monitoring and advanced anomaly detection, we can stay one step ahead of the attackers.

Remember: The best security system is one that never sleeps. By combining AI-driven monitoring, strong authentication, and proactive security measures, we can keep the grid secure, the power flowing, and the hackers frustrated.

And let's be real—if the smart grid goes down, we'll have much bigger problems than Wi-Fi outages. So let's lock it down before that happens. 🚀

10.3 Secure Firmware Updates and Patch Management Strategies

Let's be real—firmware updates are like dentist appointments. You know they're important, but you keep putting them off until something breaks (or a hacker exploits that unpatched vulnerability you ignored for months). In the smart grid world, outdated firmware is an open invitation for cybercriminals to waltz in, mess with your systems, and potentially cause blackouts.

So, unless you want a rogue hacker deciding when your city gets electricity, let's talk about how to keep firmware updated and patches properly managed—without breaking the grid in the process.

□□ Why Firmware Updates and Patch Management Matter

Smart grid systems rely on firmware to operate everything from smart meters to SCADA controllers. Unfortunately, firmware is often:

✖ **Outdated** (because updating industrial devices is a logistical nightmare)
✖ **Vulnerable** (manufacturers sometimes prioritize functionality over security)
✖ **Unpatched** (because rebooting critical infrastructure isn't always an option)

Cybercriminals love outdated firmware. It's their golden ticket to exploit known vulnerabilities, install malware, or take full control of smart grid devices.

☞ Real-world example:

In 2015, the Ukraine power grid attack leveraged vulnerabilities in unpatched industrial control systems (ICS), leading to widespread power outages affecting 225,000 people. Don't want to be the next case study? Keep that firmware updated.

🔍 Challenges in Updating Firmware and Applying Patches

⚡ 1. Downtime and Operational Disruptions

Updating a smart meter is easy. Updating an entire substation? Not so much. Power grid components are designed for continuous operation, and updates often require a reboot—which means temporary service interruptions.

☐ Solution:

✓ Implement rolling updates to minimize downtime

✓ Use redundant systems to avoid single points of failure

✓ Schedule updates during off-peak hours

☐☠☐ 2. Supply Chain Risks and Backdoored Firmware

Just because a firmware update is available doesn't mean it's safe. Attackers have been known to inject backdoors into firmware updates, compromising devices before they even reach the field.

☐ Solution:

✓ Only download updates from trusted sources

✓ Use code signing to verify firmware authenticity

✓ Conduct supply chain audits to detect tampered updates

☐ 3. Devices That Can't Be Patched

Some legacy industrial devices were never designed to be updated—because when they were built, cybersecurity wasn't a concern. These unpatchable devices are basically security time bombs waiting to be exploited.

☐ Solution:

✓ Use network segmentation to isolate vulnerable devices

✓ Deploy intrusion detection systems (IDS) to monitor for exploits

✓ Replace legacy systems wherever possible

🔑 Best Practices for Secure Firmware Updates

☐ 1. Automate Where Possible, But Maintain Control

Manually updating thousands of devices? No thanks. Automated update systems help, but they must be carefully controlled to prevent accidental deployment of faulty updates.

✅ **Best Practices:**

✓ Use centralized update management to track firmware versions

✓ Implement staged rollouts (test updates on a small group before full deployment)

✓ Require multi-factor authentication (MFA) before approving updates

🔍 2. Implement Code Signing and Cryptographic Verification

Before installing a firmware update, verify its integrity to ensure it hasn't been tampered with. Think of it like checking the security seal on a medicine bottle—if it's broken, you probably don't want to take it.

✅ **Best Practices:**

✓ Require code-signing certificates for all firmware updates

✓ Use cryptographic hashing to verify firmware integrity

✓ Implement rollback protections to prevent downgrade attacks

☐☐ 3. Air-Gapped Systems? Use Secure Offline Updates

Some smart grid components are isolated from the internet for security reasons. That's great for preventing remote attacks, but it makes updates more challenging.

✅ **Best Practices:**

✓ Use secure USB drives with hardware encryption for offline updates

✓ Verify checksum and signatures before applying updates

✓ Maintain strict access controls on who can update air-gapped systems

☐ 4. Monitor for Firmware-Based Attacks

Just because a device has the latest firmware doesn't mean it's safe. Attackers can exploit zero-day vulnerabilities, bypassing patching efforts.

✅ Best Practices:

✓ Deploy behavior-based anomaly detection to catch firmware exploits

✓ Use hardware security modules (HSMs) to protect critical firmware

✓ Conduct penetration testing to identify firmware weaknesses before attackers do

☐ Best Practices for Patch Management in Smart Grid Environments

Firmware updates are critical, but let's not forget patching software, operating systems, and network devices. Unpatched software is just as dangerous as outdated firmware.

🚀 1. Adopt a Risk-Based Patch Management Strategy

Not all patches are equally urgent. Prioritize updates based on risk level.

● **Critical vulnerabilities (exploited in the wild)** → Patch immediately

☐ **Moderate vulnerabilities (potentially exploitable)** → Patch in scheduled cycles

☐ **Low-risk patches (non-security updates)** → Deploy as needed

☐ 2. Use a Patch Management System (PMS)

Trying to track patches across thousands of devices manually? That's a recipe for disaster. A Patch Management System (PMS) automates patching while providing visibility into which systems are vulnerable.

✅ Best Practices:

✓ Deploy enterprise-grade PMS to manage updates at scale

✓ Set up automated patch testing before deployment

✓ Maintain a patch audit log for compliance tracking

□□ 3. Address Shadow IT and Rogue Devices

Sometimes, devices get deployed outside official IT control (looking at you, engineers who set up unapproved IoT devices). These shadow IT devices might never get patched, making them a serious security risk.

✅ Best Practices:

✓ Conduct regular asset discovery scans to find rogue devices

✓ Enforce patching policies across all devices

✓ Require firmware verification checks before allowing new devices on the network

♀ The Future of Secure Firmware Updates and Patch Management

□ AI-Driven Patching and Autonomous Security

Instead of relying on human intervention, AI-driven systems are emerging that can:

✅ Identify vulnerabilities in real time

✅ Automatically apply patches without downtime

✅ Predict future vulnerabilities before they become threats

□ Blockchain for Secure Firmware Updates

Some companies are experimenting with blockchain-based firmware verification, ensuring updates can't be tampered with even if a hacker breaches a manufacturer's systems.

⊚ Final Thoughts: Patch or Perish

Let's face it—patching isn't glamorous. But neither is getting hacked and causing a nationwide blackout. Keeping firmware updated and patches properly managed is non-negotiable in the smart grid world.

So, whether it's a smart meter, a SCADA system, or a substation controller, the rule is simple: patch early, patch often, and patch securely. Because the only thing worse than a system crash is knowing it could've been prevented with a simple update. 🚀

10.4 Role of AI and Machine Learning in Smart Grid Cybersecurity

Let's be honest—cybersecurity is a game of cat and mouse. Attackers find new exploits, defenders patch them, and the cycle repeats. But what if we had a super-intelligent watchdog that never sleeps, constantly monitors for threats, and predicts attacks before they even happen? That's where Artificial Intelligence (AI) and Machine Learning (ML) come in.

The smart grid is a massive, complex, and interconnected system. Traditional security methods aren't cutting it anymore—we need AI-powered defenses that learn, adapt, and fight back in real time. So, let's dive into how AI and ML are revolutionizing smart grid cybersecurity, and why it's both exciting and slightly terrifying (Skynet, anyone?).

Why AI and ML Are Game-Changers for Smart Grid Security

Smart grid infrastructure is too big, too fast, and too dynamic for human analysts alone. Attackers are using automated tools, so defenders need AI-driven solutions to keep up. Here's why AI is a cybersecurity powerhouse in the smart grid:

- **Real-time threat detection**: AI analyzes massive amounts of data and flags anomalies faster than humans.
- **Predictive analytics**: ML models can forecast potential cyber threats before they occur.
- **Automated incident response**: AI-driven systems can isolate and neutralize threats without human intervention.
- **Self-learning security**: AI continuously improves its detection capabilities based on new attack patterns.

Example:

A utility company uses an AI-powered anomaly detection system to monitor smart meters. One day, it notices an unusual spike in energy readings across multiple locations. Instead of waiting for human intervention, the AI automatically blocks suspicious traffic and alerts the security team.

AI-Powered Threat Detection and Anomaly Detection

Cyber threats in the smart grid aren't always obvious. AI can detect subtle anomalies that traditional security tools might miss.

How AI Detects Cyber Threats:

Supervised Learning: Trains AI models on past cyberattacks so they can recognize similar threats in real-time.

Unsupervised Learning: Identifies new attack patterns by detecting unusual behavior.

Reinforcement Learning: Continuously adapts and improves based on real-world cyber threats.

Example:

AI in a smart grid control center detects a SCADA system behaving slightly differently than usual. While it's not outright malicious, AI flags it as suspicious, and upon deeper inspection, it turns out to be a slow, stealthy cyberattack that human analysts would've missed.

AI and ML in Intrusion Detection and Response

When a cyberattack happens, every second counts. AI-based Intrusion Detection Systems (IDS) can:

- Detect attacks faster than traditional security tools.
- Analyze attack patterns to predict future threats.
- Trigger automated responses to neutralize threats before they cause damage.

Example: AI-Driven Automated Response

Imagine a hacker tries to execute a man-in-the-middle attack on a smart grid network. AI detects unauthorized packet injections, isolates the infected node, and reroutes traffic instantly, preventing data manipulation.

Predictive Cybersecurity: Stopping Attacks Before They Happen

Wouldn't it be great if we could stop cyberattacks before they even start? AI makes that possible by:

- Analyzing past cyber incidents to predict future attack vectors.
- Monitoring threat intelligence feeds to stay ahead of emerging threats.
- Automatically adapting security policies based on risk assessments.

Case Study: Predictive AI in Action

A utility company integrates AI into its cybersecurity system. AI analyzes past ransomware attacks, identifies high-risk entry points, and proactively hardens those systems—preventing an attack before it happens.

AI-Driven Security for Smart Grid Devices

Every device in a smart grid—from smart meters to SCADA systems—is a potential attack target. AI can monitor these devices and detect when they've been compromised.

AI Securing Smart Grid Endpoints:

- **Behavioral Analysis**: AI monitors smart meters and detects unusual energy usage patterns that might indicate fraud.
- **Self-Healing Devices**: AI enables automatic rollback to secure firmware if a device is compromised.
- **Zero-Trust Security**: AI enforces strict access controls, ensuring that only trusted entities can communicate within the grid.

AI and Machine Learning in Network Security

Smart grids rely on complex communication networks that are constantly under attack. AI helps by:

- **Identifying network anomalies** (e.g., unexpected data flows).
- **Detecting insider threats** (e.g., rogue employees modifying grid parameters).

- Preventing DDoS attacks by rate-limiting malicious traffic.

Case Study: AI Defending Against a DDoS Attack

Attackers flood a utility company's AMI (Advanced Metering Infrastructure) with fake traffic to disrupt billing services. AI instantly identifies the malicious traffic and blocks it before it takes down the system.

Challenges and Ethical Considerations in AI-Driven Security

AI isn't perfect. It can make mistakes, misidentify threats, and even be exploited by attackers. Here are the biggest challenges:

- **Bias in AI models**: If trained on biased data, AI might incorrectly label normal behavior as a cyberattack.
- **False positives**: AI security tools sometimes flag harmless activity, causing unnecessary shutdowns.
- **Adversarial AI attacks**: Hackers can trick AI models into ignoring real threats.

The Future of AI in Smart Grid Cybersecurity

AI is evolving fast, and the future of smart grid cybersecurity is looking both promising and terrifying (Skynet, please don't take over). Some key trends to watch:

AI-Powered Autonomous Cyber Defense: AI will become fully autonomous, detecting and responding to cyber threats without human intervention.
Blockchain + AI Security: Combining AI with blockchain will ensure that grid communications remain tamper-proof.
Quantum AI Security: AI-powered quantum encryption could make smart grid networks unhackable (at least until quantum hackers show up).

Final Thoughts: AI is the Future of Smart Grid Security

AI isn't just a cool buzzword—it's the future of cybersecurity in smart grids. It helps predict, detect, and neutralize cyber threats in ways that traditional security tools can't match. But AI isn't a magic bullet—it still requires human oversight and continuous improvement.

So, if you want to keep your smart grid secure, embrace AI-driven cybersecurity—or prepare to battle AI-powered hackers on your own. (Spoiler: they don't take coffee breaks.)

10.5 Future Trends and Challenges in Smart Grid Protection

Let's be real—the smart grid is getting smarter, but so are the hackers. As we race toward a future filled with AI-driven automation, decentralized energy systems, and next-gen wireless tech, cybercriminals are just as eager to exploit every shiny new upgrade.

In this final chapter, we'll dive into the biggest trends shaping smart grid security and the challenges that lie ahead. Spoiler alert: it's a never-ending battle. But hey, what's cybersecurity without a little adrenaline rush?

The Future of Smart Grid Protection: What's Coming Next?

Smart grids are evolving fast, and with great power (literally) comes great responsibility. Here are some key trends that will shape smart grid security in the coming years:

AI-Driven Cybersecurity & Automated Threat Response

We're moving toward self-defending smart grids, where AI and machine learning detect, analyze, and neutralize cyber threats in real-time.

Future Possibilities:

AI-powered anomaly detection that instantly isolates compromised grid components.

Self-healing networks that reroute power flows in case of a cyberattack.

Automated security patching to fix vulnerabilities before attackers exploit them.

Challenge: AI itself can be hacked! Adversarial AI attacks could manipulate security algorithms, making AI think everything's fine—when it's not.

Blockchain for Smart Grid Security

Decentralization isn't just for crypto nerds anymore. Blockchain can secure smart grid transactions by ensuring data integrity, tamper-proof logs, and transparent access control.

How Blockchain Will Help:

Prevent data manipulation in smart meter readings and energy transactions.

Secure vehicle-to-grid (V2G) communications for EV charging stations.

Enable smart contracts for automated, trustless energy trading.

Challenge: Blockchain scalability is still an issue—smart grids process massive amounts of data, and blockchain-based solutions need to keep up without slowing things down.

5G and Edge Computing: The New Attack Frontier

Faster networks and edge computing = better performance, right? Yes—but also more security headaches.

Why 5G & Edge Computing Matter:

Ultra-fast, low-latency communication enables real-time smart grid operations.

Edge computing reduces dependence on centralized cloud servers, improving efficiency.

Devices process data locally, making smart grids more resilient to network disruptions.

Challenge: With billions of edge devices, attack surfaces multiply. If attackers compromise an edge node, they can manipulate local grid operations without triggering alarms in the central system.

Quantum Computing: The Ultimate Cybersecurity Nightmare?

Quantum computing is the boogeyman of encryption—a fully operational quantum computer could break today's encryption standards in minutes.

How Smart Grid Security Must Adapt:

Transitioning to quantum-resistant encryption algorithms (a.k.a. post-quantum cryptography).

Developing hybrid security models that can withstand quantum decryption attacks.

Researching quantum-safe blockchain protocols to keep distributed energy transactions secure.

Challenge: We don't know when quantum computers will become a real threat, but when they do, every existing encryption method will be at risk.

Cyber-Physical Attack Simulations & Digital Twins

Security testing will move beyond traditional penetration testing—we'll see more realistic cyber-physical attack simulations using digital twins.

What's a Digital Twin?

It's a virtual replica of a smart grid system that allows security teams to:

- Simulate cyberattacks in a safe environment.
- Test new defense strategies without disrupting the actual grid.
- Train AI-powered security models to respond to real-world threats.

Challenge: Building accurate digital twins is complex and expensive, but the benefits far outweigh the costs.

Biggest Cybersecurity Challenges Facing Smart Grids

While new technologies promise better security, cybercriminals aren't backing down. Here are the biggest challenges we must overcome:

1. Increasing Attack Surfaces

The more connected devices, the more entry points for attackers. From smart meters to EV charging stations, attackers have more ways to infiltrate the grid.

Solution: Zero-trust security models that verify every device before granting access.

2. Insider Threats & Supply Chain Attacks

Sometimes, the biggest threats come from within. Whether it's a disgruntled employee or a compromised vendor, insider attacks are harder to detect.

Solution: AI-powered behavioral monitoring to identify suspicious activities within the grid network.

3. Lack of Standardized Security Frameworks

Different regions follow different smart grid security standards (NERC CIP, IEC 62443, ISO 27019). This lack of global consistency creates gaps in security enforcement.

Solution: Push for global security standards and ensure compliance with multiple frameworks.

4. Cyber-Physical Risks and Blackout Scenarios

A cyberattack on a power grid isn't just about stealing data—it can cause blackouts, equipment failures, and even physical destruction.

Solution: Build fail-safe mechanisms so that even if attackers gain access, the grid can self-heal and restore operations.

Final Thoughts: The Future is Both Exciting & Terrifying

We're standing at the edge of a new era in smart grid security. The good news? We have AI, blockchain, and quantum-resistant encryption to help protect our energy systems. The bad news? Attackers have access to AI, blockchain, and quantum hacking tools too.

At the end of the day, cybersecurity is a war of innovation—whoever adapts the fastest wins. So, if you're working in smart grid security, stay sharp, keep learning, and never stop questioning "what's next?"

Because in the future of cybersecurity, the only constant is change.

Well, here we are at the end of our deep dive into **Smart Grid Cybersecurity: Attacking and Defending Energy IoT Systems**. If you've made it this far, congratulations! You now know more about hacking the power grid than most people ever will (just, you know, use this knowledge for good, not for turning your city into a scene from Mad Max). We've covered everything from reconnaissance and attack surface mapping to exploiting AMI networks, attacking SCADA systems, and messing with EV charging stations—all while laughing through the terrifying reality of how vulnerable our energy infrastructure really is.

The smart grid is a fascinating, chaotic, and sometimes horrifying blend of old-school industrial systems and modern IoT technologies, and as we've seen, it's far from bulletproof. But that's exactly why we need people like you—ethical hackers, security researchers, and defenders—to stay one step ahead of the bad guys. This isn't just about protecting infrastructure; it's about protecting modern civilization itself. If that doesn't make you feel like a cyber superhero, I don't know what will.

What's Next? Keep Hacking, Keep Learning!

If this book got you excited about breaking and securing critical systems, then guess what? There's a whole world of IoT hacking waiting for you! This book is part of my IoT Red Teaming: Offensive and Defensive Strategies series, which means there's plenty more cyber mayhem to explore. Want to hack smart vehicles? Check out The Car Hacker's Guide. Curious about breaking into Wi-Fi, Bluetooth, and RF protocols? You'll love Wireless Hacking Unleashed. If medical devices or satellites sound more your speed, we've got Hacking Medical IoT and Satellite Hacking to keep you busy. Basically, if it's connected and exploitable, I've probably written about it.

Gratitude: You're the Real MVP!

I just want to take a moment to say—thank you. Seriously. Writing these books is a wild ride, but knowing that people like you are out there, learning, hacking, and making the world a safer place, makes it all worth it. Cybersecurity is a never-ending battle, and it's people like you who keep pushing the field forward. So keep testing, keep questioning, and most importantly, keep securing the things that matter—because trust me, there are plenty of things left to fix.

Until next time, stay curious, stay ethical, and as always… hack the system, defend the grid, and don't let the bad guys win.

– *Zephyrion Stravos*